It's the details that make a home feel special.
Join Steffy Degreff as she invites you on a year-long
tour of her thoughtfully designed living spaces—
an A-frame cabin in the Catskill Mountains and a
modern family home in Long Beach, New York. You'll
learn how to use decorative elements to create a
home that feels cozy and inviting.

For each month of the year, Steffy shares styling tips
to reflect the seasonal changes and showcase your
personal aesthetic, from the addition of whimsical
vintage pieces to a spring table setting or mini
pumpkins placed around a room in creative ways for
fall. Enhance both the interior and exterior of your
home with twenty-five DIY projects including
everything from hanging flowers to cabinet wreaths.

Whether you live in a cabin in the woods, a high-rise
in the city, or a duplex in the burbs, *A Home for Every
Season* provides inspiration and guidance for making
your space festive year-round. **Welcome home.**

A HOME FOR EVERY SEASON

A HOME FOR EVERY SEASON

A MONTH-BY-MONTH GUIDE TO DECORATING YOUR SPACE

STEFFY DEGREFF

PHOTOGRAPHY BY NICK GLIMENAKIS

DK

Publisher Mike Sanders
Senior Editor Alexander Rigby
Art Director William Thomas
Senior Designer Jessica Lee
Photographer Nick Glimenakis
Styling Assistant Sea D'Amico
Proofreaders Emma Chance, Lisa Starnes
Recipe Tester Robert Naugle III
Indexer Johnna VanHoose Dinse

First American Edition, 2023
Published in the United States by DK Publishing
6081 E 82nd St, Suite 400, Indianapolis, IN 46250

Library of Congress Catalog Number: 2023931548
ISBN 978-0-7440-7743-8

DK books are available at
special discounts when purchased
in bulk for sales promotions, premiums,
fund-raising, or educational use. For details,
contact SpecialSales@dk.com

Printed and bound in China

For the curious
www.dk.com

This book was made with Forest
Stewardship Council ™ certified
paper - one small step in DK's
commitment to a sustainable future.
For more information go to
www.dk.com/our-green-pledge

DEDICATION

To my dad, for instilling in me a love for homes
and the confidence to make my home my own.

CONTENTS

INTRODUCTION

Define "normal" to me. I would argue we all have our peculiarities, some more obvious than others. Mine is evident as soon as you step into my home—I take seasonal décor very, very seriously. This peculiarity of mine started out in small ways, then snowballed into something that felt beyond my control, and then impossible to stop. What began with a few pumpkins on my stoop and some faux garlands around the doorframe in October continued to grow over the years, and now the universe would seem imbalanced if my door color didn't match the feeling of every season. This is my way of living.

So when I was approached to write this book about how I use seasonal décor in my A-frame home in March 2022, I knew I had to share what it looked like over the course of a full year, with the hope that my way of living could inspire some of you. I chose to include my main home in Long Beach as well, since I also pour hours into decorating it seasonally. It is a more typical style of home that relates to the way most people live. A-frames are sort of like mythical creatures, you rarely ever meet someone who lives in them full-time!

We began the first shoot when the flowers bloomed in spring 2022, timing it around the cherry blossom tree in the front yard of the A-frame. So we technically started shooting the photos for this book somewhere in the middle. We continued working throughout the summer, shooting the next chapters in July, the day after my 35th birthday. It was a classic summer weekend in the Catskills that included bonfires, dips in the nearby swimming hole, and a full house: from DK Publishing's team, to my management team, and our photographer, who all travelled up to the A-frame for the affair.

The fall shoots happened to land on two days of nonstop rain. We stood out in front of the house suited up in rain jackets with the camera covered in a poncho as we aimed to capture the magic of fall. Leaves covered absolutely every inch of the ground around us. It was an unforgettable week—the same week Taylor Swift's *Midnights* album was released—which we played over and over again while capturing the images. The holiday chapter was shot in early December on a beautiful, brisk, short day. We had to start snapping photos right at sunrise, as the days are laughably short in December, and we lost most of our light inside by 3 p.m.

For the final shoot, which ended up being the photos the book opens with, we wanted to catch a blizzard in January. Our vision was to see the A-frame completely covered in fresh powder, but with the weather being unseasonably warm, we hadn't seen any snow yet. I noticed the weather forecast called for two days of snow starting on January 22, so we took a chance on those days, making the three hour drive up to the A-frame with our fingers and toes crossed. On the morning of January 23rd, I woke up at sunrise to the most incredible winter wonderland—a perfect snow day for the final shoot that would begin the book.

And now, as I sit here writing this, I am pulling out my spring décor, as I patiently wait for the cherry blossoms to bloom once again. The seasons keep showing up, year after year, whether we're ready for them to come or not. (I'm talking to you, winter!) My hope is that if you're feeling uninspired or lost as a new season approaches, you'll reach for this book, and it will reinvigorate you to embrace the changes that happen, even if they feel out of your control. Grab some paint, build something, bake some seasonal cookies, and take a few hours with your thoughts to reflect!

BUYING THE A-FRAME

My A-frame story begins when I was a little girl. Twelve, to be exact. My dad, always a dreamer and an old car fanatic, drove us to a Volkswagen dealership to check out a camper van. The exact color of the van itself is hazy, but I can remember my dad's energy, that wholesome smile on his face, the look of a man who was maybe going to fulfill a lifelong bucket list item. We entered the van and stood in its kitchen space, narrow, but with everything we'd need to cook food on the open road. I had never been in a car with a kitchen before, and I thought it was so cool. My brothers and I chimed in, "Let's get it!"

We left that day without the van, but I learned something that changed the way I chose to live my life from that moment forward: I would be the kind of person who indulges in the things in adulthood that I dreamt of doing when I was little. I would find a way to be the mom who gets the camper van, and makes memories using it. And that is without throwing shade at my parents, because as a 12-year-old, I couldn't understand their financial situation or the many reasons why they didn't get that 1999 van. I just knew that the expression on my dad's face was something special. The childhood excitement something like a dream vehicle could pull out of him . . . it was a feeling I would chase in my own life.

Fast forward to March of 2018 when my husband drove home with our very own 1977 Toyota Ponte-X from Vermont. It was the length of a standard truck, and it fit into a parking spot, but it had two beds and a full kitchen: the perfect size for our small family of three. Our son Hudson, who was almost two years old at the time, would sleep in the top bed, and my husband Matt and I would squeeze into a twin bed to make it work. We spent a few months fixing up the van, ripping out the weird spray foam ceilings and

waterlogged flooring, adding vibrant orange curtains, and putting in new beige waterproof floors with vertical white lines from the front to back of the van. I used peel and stick wood look-alike countertops in the kitchen for a trendier look, and painted the cabinets white. We spent two fall seasons exploring Upstate New York, sleeping amongst the orange foliage, squished into that twin bed. We'd cook pasta for dinner and eat sitting at the table (which was transformed from our bed) beneath the string lights we'd strung along the interior. One of our favorite trips was to an A-frame that was part of a boutique hotel called Lokal about fifty minutes from Philadelphia on the Maurice River. Even though it wasn't easy to travel with a toddler in a small van, Matt and I both felt like it was fulfilling our thirst for adventure, which we never stopped craving.

In March of 2020, our second son Charlie was born, and his arrival changed everything. As most parents know, it's much easier to pick up and go with one kid, but having a second child changes your entire world. Days went by, which turned into weeks, and before we knew it, we hadn't used our van in over six months. It just didn't work with a newborn and a toddler together, and we knew deep down it was time to let go of the dream. On August 10th, 2020, we found a buyer for the van, and it wrecked me. I felt like saying goodbye to the van was a loss of my own childhood, and the acceptance that my life now revolved around what was right for and worked best for my children. The camper van no longer fit us. We had outgrown it. I spent the next few months wondering what was next and how I'd keep the same kind of energy my dad once brought to the camper van lot alive. I wanted to find a way to carry it onward into our changed world now that we had two kids.

During 2020 I found myself—like every other person on TikTok and Instagram—redecorating and DIYing my home. I installed peel and stick wallpaper in our entryway, painted accent walls (not once, but twice when the green color wasn't just right!) and taught myself how to work with some power tools to install a board and batten wall next to my closet. In October of 2020, two months after selling our van, I took a three-day trip to The Alpine A-frame in Wilmington, Vermont. It stands out from other A-frames because the outside is painted a bright teal blue. You cannot miss it, no matter the time of year. Before this trip, I had stayed at a slew of other A-frames, including the Lokal and a few others in Hunter, New York, we visited with our van. On one morning of the trip, I woke up early and drove to the local farmstand, picked up almond milk, coffee, and some eggs to make at home for my friend Noelle and me. As I cooked in the cute little kitchen, grabbing bowls off the open shelf above the stove, I thought: this is something I want to do all of the time. Wake up in a cozy A-frame bedroom, cook eggs from a small local farm, and spend nights with my family around the fire.

This could be my next passion project.

I've always been drawn to the charm of an A-frame. Most of them have a fireplace right in the center of the living room, the only room available to sit and play games or listen to music with friends and family. The layout of the home brings people together, and elicits feelings of nostalgia. You can just envision the families before you doing the exact same thing in the same tiny living room back in the 70s and the 80s, enjoying their vacations in the woods. These homes are also often a work in progress. There's so much room to revive them, bring them back to life, modernize them, and DIY them. I was attracted by how so many of these A-frames had the potential to be even better than they already were. I would always walk away after a rental stay with so many ideas on how I would have done things differently. Some were already beautiful and redone (like Lokal!) while others I've stayed in had old, stained carpeting, and walls that were itching to be removed to let more light in.

For Christmas 2020, one of Matt's gifts to me was an embroidered A-frame, and I placed it in my closet. I'd look at it in the morning while I was getting dressed. If there's one thing I believe in, it is manifestation, and manifesting this one did not let me down.

Less than two months after I received that gift, we were staying in an Airbnb rental in Upstate New York when I saw an Instagram post from a local realtor about an A-frame for sale. I googled the address, and it was only 12 minutes from where we were staying. It felt like it was meant to be. We had been casually looking, but because we lived a few hours away from most properties upstate, we hadn't been able to go to any showings. Most homes were selling in a few days. We knew by this point if we were ever going to make our A-frame dream a reality, it would have to be the perfect timing. We decided to jump at this chance. I called the realtor, and before I hung up, Matt was on the phone with our mortgage broker to get a pre-approval. We were all set to wake up the next morning and walk through the house!

It's a day I will never forget. My boys were four and ten months old. It was one of those gorgeous winter days where the air was crisp, but the speckled sunlight trickled through the trees and made us feel warm. We anxiously took the 12-minute drive toward Phoenicia, passed our favorite diner, and headed uphill—where all cell service cuts out—and made our way down the long snowy quarter-mile driveway.

As we drove up, I saw it for the very first time. The sun flared from behind the triangle roofline as I stepped out of the car and strapped Charlie into his carrier. The house was a greyish purple color, with large, aggressive black mats leading up to the front door. My first thought was how beautiful the property was—a half acre of land with a gazebo, a shed, and a built-in fire pit. I could see us growing old here. My second thought after walking inside was *damn, this house is dark.* Being the kind of person who really needs some sort of natural light, it was worrisome to me. I always thought that a lack of natural light was a deal breaker, but every other thing about the home was just right. The wood was in pristine condition, the bathroom was fully functional, and aesthetics aside (and many other issues we'd discover later on), it was move-in ready. The bones were good! Right then and there, we put in an offer. It felt really scary, but it also felt right. We soon found out that many other people also saw themselves growing old there, and we realized we had to up our offer above asking price and send a personal note.

After a week of waiting and tons of back-and-forth calls with the realtor, we got the call that the owner had selected us! Matt and I got incredibly excited like we always do when crazy-good life news comes along. We looked at each other and said, "Can you believe we're going to own an A-frame?!" We felt like excited little kids—just like how my dad had felt that day at the camper van lot.

RENOVATION

On March 22, 2021, we woke up our kids before sunrise, packed the car, and made the three-hour drive upstate to officially become the owners of an A-frame. There was still a bit of snow on the ground, but it was the second day of spring, and it was warm enough to get away with wearing a light coat and a beanie. The closing felt hopeful and exciting, like a fresh start after a really wild 2020 that was spent inside avoiding COVID with a newborn. One of the big stipulations of the purchase was that the previous owner was leaving all her belongings at the house. It was an as-is purchase. We were never able to meet her, but seeing as this was her second home, it seemed she was unable to empty it out, or just didn't want the burden of it all. We were eager and unphased by the challenge, but once we had the keys in-hand, it suddenly felt like a much larger job. Emptying out the A-frame was the first of many hurdles we bumped into headfirst, but we went in with an action plan and were ready to get rid of a lot of things!

We spent the first few weeks as A-frame owners pulling up rugs, going through every cabinet, and making piles for donations and piles for the garbage dump. We wanted to try and make the house feel empty enough to renovate. There were some things about buying an as-is home that were great: the previous owner had left her beds, so we could sleep in the home without running out and buying mattresses right away, and the kitchen was completely functional from day one, with pots, pans, silverware, plates, etc. Before your brain goes there, the mattresses were clean, and the previous owner was trustworthy, so we were not nervous to use the old beds at all! But truth be told, the negatives far outweighed the positives in walking into a house completely filled with someone else's belongings. Luckily, the weather was in the fifties as we cut down rugs with an exacto blade out

front, and broke them down enough to take them to the garbage dump. We listed a dozen pieces of furniture for free on Facebook and Craigslist. People stopped by to collect items throughout the day in between our trips to the dump. In the first two days alone, we gave away a couch, a coffee table, a rollaway cart, a portable washing machine, mason jars, lamps, and tons of wicker baskets—the previous owner had a thing for wicker baskets.

We also took old curtains and curtain rods to the dump, along with insulation and nonfunctioning equipment in the shed. There was a built-in desk we had to demo and throw off the second floor balcony. We even had a few weird situations come up in the process of giving things away. I accidentally jumbled our address over Facebook Marketplace, and when nobody showed up to pick up the washer, I offered it to someone else who swooped in to grab it right away. An hour later, a man with the wrong address messaged to say he had been circling around our neighborhood without phone service. When he found out someone else had picked up the washer in the meantime, he was not happy, even though I had messaged him to let him know I was giving it to someone else an hour prior.

Once the house was mostly empty (aside from the Lay-Z-Boy that we kept in place of a couch for far too long), I began to tackle the smaller fixes and came up with a plan and an order for all of the larger renovations. We had an inspection done before we closed, but one of the biggest lessons we learned fairly quickly was that an inspection report only goes so far, and the term "good bones" can sometimes gloss over a lot of very expensive flaws. In our case, the first big thing we learned was the fact that the home had radon in it, which we actually did find out from the inspection. It ended up being a bit costly to install a radon mitigation system, and while the installer was down in the crawl space below our house putting this in, he stumbled upon something else we needed to fix we weren't prepared for: the amount of humidity in our crawl space. So our next invisible cost (as I call them—costs for things that add comfort, but nothing aesthetically pleasing to a home) was for a whole-house dehumidifier system, also to be located in the crawl space. The third very large fix we discovered was our roof, which had been listed as at its "half-life" in the inspection report. My dad, who is a general contractor, noticed right away that it needed to be replaced sooner, especially if we wanted to add skylights, which we did.

Before jumping into large fixes, we started with the smaller ones. I spent many pajama-clad mornings unscrewing things like the rusty shower curtain rod and pulling down kitchen cabinetry to open up the space a bit. Because of some of the expenses we weren't prepared to spend money on, we decided to cut corners in other places by DIYing certain things, which was a great way to save money. The plan was to film the DIY projects for my TikTok, which would be a fun way to keep people as excited about the A-frame transformation as I was! I kept seeing videos of people painting over their tile and stenciling it. I thought this would be a great project to start in our downstairs bathroom. The current tile had a very outdated vinyl look to it, but the rest of the bathroom wasn't in bad shape. There were cute subway tiles in the shower, as well as a retro pedestal sink and a functioning toilet. So the only true piece that felt like it didn't fit in with my style was the tile floor. I did a lot of research, and then I spent three days tackling the project. The most time-consuming piece about stenciling a floor is the dry time in between layers, so I made a day trip with my son Hudson to put on the first coat of white primer. We left our Long Beach

home at 8 a.m., arrived at the A-frame at 11 a.m., and then were back on the road to Long Beach at 6 p.m. It was a long day of driving and painting (and peeing in the woods; I totally spaced on the fact that this bathroom was our only one!), but it prepped me for the second step, the actual stenciling. I came back with my assistant Sea and my best friend Noelle, and we drank red wine and tested out different methods of how to roll versus blot paint in a stencil. After a glass of wine and a lot of begging from my friends to not start the project, I decided at 10 p.m. that I would just test a few tiles. It was so invigorating, and I couldn't believe what a huge difference the stencil made to the space! It was my first taste of a true space-altering DIY, and the next day I spent hours hunched over the floor stenciling. I had moments of panic, thinking I had messed up or blew it, but Noelle kept saying "the mistakes just give it character!" to which I wholeheartedly disagreed. But in the end, my biggest realization was that it was just paint, and it could easily be fixed by adding more paint. I kept this mentality with the rest of our DIYs, since a lot of them pushed me outside my comfort zone, working with tools and mediums I had never worked with before. The floor ended up coming out amazing, and the bathroom looked like an entirely new space.

I then jumped into painting the entire A-frame white with Sea's help. We started by painting the downstairs first. We drove up and stayed for two days with a plan to basically paint from morning until night. It sounded fun (okay, maybe not fun to everyone, but for us it was), and we were so excited to watch the space brighten up before our eyes, but by hour eight, we were entirely exhausted. I had never painted a ceiling, and phew, is it an arm workout! We had Morrisey blasting, and the neighbors kept walking up the driveway to see what we were up to. All of the long hours spent in the A-frame with the double doors open to let the sunshine in started to make the place feel more like my own. We used a Zinser

shellac-based primer for the first two coats to cover up the knotty pine, and then we painted two coats of Clare Paint in Fresh Kicks, a bright and warm-colored white. The space was completely transformed by the end of those two days. We came back up two weeks later at the end of May to tackle painting the upstairs, and we enlisted the help of my younger brother Matt, who ended up being more of a coffee-fetcher and less of a "grab a paintbrush and paint" kind of guy. For some reason, we thought the upstairs would be easier, but it was not. The high ceilings made it even tougher than the downstairs, and the weekend we chose to paint ended up being one of the warmest that spring. We were roasting, it must have been close to 85°F (29°C) inside. Tensions were high, quarters were tight, and time was of the essence, but we somehow got the entire upstairs painted in three days. When we finished, we treated ourselves to a delicious meal at Cucina in Woodstock, with paint still splattered on our hands.

Even with the new bright-white paint, the house was still dark and felt like the inside of a ship since it lacked natural light. But on June 1st, everything changed! And because of this, I still stand firm in calling this one of my favorite days, just behind my wedding day and the births of my two kids. At 9 a.m. a crew of around twenty-five guys showed up and started to demo our old roof. Renovating the roof on an A-frame is more challenging than any other type of home since there's nowhere flat for the men to work. Some men were sitting all the way up at the peak of the roofline with one foot on the left side of the roof and one foot on the right, while others attached a rope that they buckled themselves on to while they scaled the side of the house as if they were rock climbing. It was an unbelievable sight to see. It took the guys only half the day to rip the entire roof off, and then the true fun began! Our roof was rotted out on half the home, so they ended up having to rip all the plywood out and replace it. I walked around the house with blue painters' tape and taped off where each skylight would be placed. We were adding in nine! The addition of so many windows was controversial amongst the building department, and we even had to get an architect's approval, but these nine skylights completely transformed the entire home, and brought the outdoors in. We used VELUX

no-leak solar powered skylights. We added three to the living room, one to the kitchen above the sink, one to the downstairs bedroom, three upstairs, and then one special skylight for egress upstairs. I proudly watched as they cut out the holes in the A-frame one by one, and framed in the new skylights. I kept thinking *this is what real joy feels like.* I know some people feel that kind of joy from a really good meal, or a great book, but this was it for me!

At the end of the day, they tarped the house for the night. They continued on the second day by finishing up adding the second-floor skylights and adding the shingles to the roof. The roofer told me at the end of the job that this was one of the most impactful before and after transformations he had seen. I was basking in the natural light, and also starting to plan so many other projects now that the house was bright enough for taking photos and videos! Next up was the kitchen renovation, which I planned to DIY.

One of the most common questions I get asked about the A-frame is why we decided to DIY our kitchen when we were investing so much in every other area. The truth is, I didn't hate the current kitchen as it

was. I liked the layout overall, and felt it was mostly as good as it would get for the space. The cabinets were nice-quality wood, and the storage space was exactly what we needed for a home that was never going to be our full-time space. We thought about pulling the countertops off and replacing them, but we feared that if we did that, there was a chance we'd wreck the cabinets in the process and end up having to rip everything out. The kitchen is original to the home, and we weren't sure how much renovation the cabinets could take. It felt like we could do more harm than good by trying to rip out certain pieces and not others. Because of this fear, we chose to DIY all of it. The first step was to DIY the countertops using a marble countertop paint kit from Giani Marble. I researched the kit, and it had all great reviews. Have I ever painted marble before? Absolutely not. Was I scared shitless? You bet! I think painting white primer directly onto my kitchen countertops has to be one of the scariest things I've ever done, but in my mind, the worst-case scenario would be having to rip everything up. The painting process took two days, plus seven days of curing time. I started by priming the countertops, then I hand painted marble look-alike veining in grey paint directly onto the white surface. It dried overnight, and then in the morning, I epoxied the countertops, which I had also never done. Epoxy is self-leveling, so aside from pouring it out, all I had to do was make sure that any gaps or bubbles were filled in. I also prepped tremendously by taping up plastic all under the cabinets and inside of the sink for any epoxy that might drip over the edges. I left the space for a week, and during that time the countertops cured and hardened. I could not believe how realistic the marble looked when it was finished. I wouldn't have known they were painted on if I hadn't done it myself!

On my birthday weekend in July, I took a day to paint the cabinets. I had painted cabinets before in a much larger kitchen, so it actually felt like a really fun, nonstressful job with a huge payoff. The color I chose was a warm, dark green, and it completely transformed the kitchen. I unscrewed the cabinets and painted them outside near the gazebo, then I brought them inside the gazebo so the wind wouldn't blow any leaves or dirt onto them as they dried. The cabinet color was the one DIY that had my husband

in shock. He could not believe how beautiful the kitchen looked! We also swapped out our fridge for a new SMEG and upgraded our cabinet knobs and faucet. A lot of small changes made a huge impact. When we were done, it felt like we had an entirely new kitchen.

Another month went by, and I somehow convinced my dad to devote a few days to helping us rip out the deck in front of the house and insulate our crawl space before winter. I felt bad inviting him to stay, mostly because he is 6'4" and the bed in our second bedroom is small. He was also sharing a room with my 1-year-old son, who would wake him up at the crack of dawn. The A-frame is not great for guests because of its size, but my dad is like me: hyperfocused on the project at hand, and willing to help with anything. He spent the first day tearing down the deck with Matt's help as my older son yelled up to him, "Grandpa, don't die up there!" The second day, we all took turns underneath the house, measuring for the framing, making cuts, and installing the insulation down below to make sure the home wouldn't freeze over during the winter ahead.

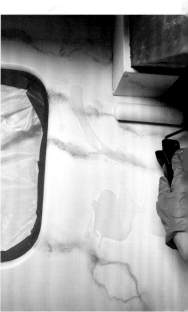

Once the deck was removed out front, we were able to swap out all the original windows and doors for brand new ones. On October 1st, a crew of six men showed up with our new windows and doors, and it took them less than a day to remove and replace everything! The most exciting change came from the addition of our triangle window upstairs in the main bedroom. It was originally a door that led out to the balcony, and once the triangle window was installed, we actually had wall space to push our bed's headboard up against. It completely transformed the room. The new French doors in the front of the house were painted a custom black on the outside, and white on the inside. They added an updated, modern feeling to the front of the home. The final step of the transformation was the outside paint color, which we deliberated over for a long time. I photoshopped every color under the sun onto the home, and there were a few runner-ups in particular that we really liked in our selection journey. We loved the idea of a black A-frame but felt it was too common. A dark, upstate green was also in contention, but we were worried that it might blend into the trees around it, and we really wanted our home to pop! Then we remembered an A-frame cabin that we snapped a film photo of five years earlier in Iceland. It was a warm orange shade, blanketed in snow.

It ended up being the inspiration for the color of our home, and our final push to take the leap, and paint the house a bright orange. We envisioned it working in all seasons—a bright pop of warmth while blanketed in snow, a vibrant color to pair with the blooming flowers in spring, a fresh-squeezed citrus vibe in the summer, and a beautiful autumnal backdrop when the leaves change. The week before Halloween, the house was painted in two days, with the peak fall leaves surrounding it. Our A-frame finally became everything we had dreamed of!

Once all the large and small renovations were completed, we were able to focus on finding the right furniture and home décor for the space. From sourcing our beautiful velvet couch, to finding a metal bed frame for the main bedroom upstairs, this was the fun part! As the house became a home and the space filled up with chairs, tables, and new mattresses, my attention began to turn to my favorite piece of the puzzle: the seasonal home décor! And it just so happens that's when I was approached to write this book. The timing felt so serendipitous. It was meant to be—my first year fully decorating my new home, and a book to follow what that journey looked like.

WINTER

Everything has a beginning, a middle, and an end. For those of us who live in places in the northern hemisphere, the beginning of each year always consists of some of the coldest, snowiest days, forcing us indoors to experience long hours of solitude (or making us go stir crazy, with kids running around). For some, this brings a longing for warmer months, less layers, and more days spent outside in the sun, but I try to accept these days with their opportunities for alone time. (Notice I did not say loneliness!) This time of year allows us to take a step back from the world after the socially exhausting holiday parties are over and cuddle up with a good book or movie. As a new year kicks off, I find myself watching the snow fall out the window, spinning a record, lighting a candle, or making soup. Winter can be magical and cozy if you lean into it and put on some really warm layers.

Gilmore Girls is a show that captures this season perfectly. During winter, I often think about the scene where Lorelai Gilmore runs outside frantically in the middle of the night because it's the first snow. She grabs her robe, takes a deep breath, and says "I smell snow." Seconds later, she stands still and takes in the feeling of watching the flurries fall all around her as the world goes completely silent. On the morning of our winter photo shoot during the first major snowfall of the season at the A-frame, I woke up with the sun at 6:50 a.m., grabbed my Blundstones and my warmest coat, and went on a two-mile walk off-the-grid with no cell service, all by myself. The world was peaceful and quiet, the only noise coming from the soft, padding sounds of snowflakes landing on the ground all around me. A few happy tears fell from my eyes. Winter might be cold, but seeing the world blanketed in white is worth the chapped lips and red cheeks every single year.

One of the most beautiful parts of an Upstate New York snowstorm is seeing my driveway blanketed in white. In the first few hours after the snow falls, the snow stays perfectly intact, sitting atop all the trees' branches.

JANUARY

The ball drops, and whether you're awake until midnight or not, you'll be opening your eyes to a brand new year on the morning of January 1st. You may lie in bed feeling sad to end what was a wonderful year, which may make you feel a bit overwhelmed as you wonder how you'll be able to top it. Or maybe it's the complete opposite, and you couldn't wait for the year to end. The unknowns and blank slate of a new year can feel exciting. Some of you might not even care about a new year—it's just a number on a calendar that ultimately feels similar to every year prior. Regardless of where you land, you'll roll out of bed, brush your teeth for the first time of the year, and decide whether to keep doing things the same way you've been doing them or try to approach things a bit differently. Maybe you'll drive a new way to work, or you'll stress clean your house and donate 10 bags of clothes and toys to Goodwill. Maybe you'll join a new workout class, or you'll end a friendship that dragged you down during the year that came before. You might realize you need a few weeks to just stay home and cook tons of tasty meals, go to bed early, and not consume alcohol for the entire month.

I've probably tried all of these things, and to be honest, none of them have been life-altering. But what they have done is gotten me through the month of January, a sometimes very quiet, cold, dark month that can often feel long and never-ending. For me, starting something new is half of the battle, and I feel that way at the start of each year. By February or March, I've found my groove, but in January I am often idling, trying to understand who I ended the year prior as and how far away she is from the person I actually want to be.

The orange shade of our home is always bright, but it shines brightest when it's enveloped in a fresh, white snow!

COZY TEXTURES

There are a few must-haves for a snowy day: a warm fire burning inside, a good book to cozy up with, some fresh ground coffee, and an endless amount of blankets, pillows, and textures to get comfortable with. January is for neutrals, whites, creams, sherpa, and knits. I love to cover my couch with blankets that invite you to wrap yourself up in and take a nap. I enjoy stripping my space down to remove the overwhelming holiday décor and lean into that empty, clean look with just a few sparse pieces that are more understated. The living room of the A-frame mirrors the white powder covering the grounds outside, and it couldn't feel any cozier.

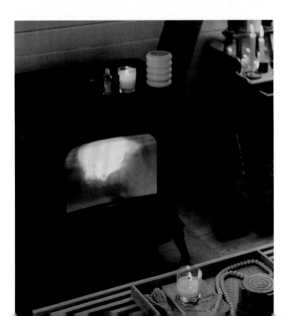

WARM LIGHTS FOR COLD DAYS

If you're going to be stuck inside, then make the inside feel like magic! I love to keep white lights hung up for January and add textures on top of textures. Add knit blankets and fur blankets to your space. You can never have too many blankets during the first month of the year. The goal is to never want to leave the comfort of bed because, let's be honest, on a lot of days that remain below 20°F (-7°C), I barely leave. Lining the overhead wood beams with warm lights helps give this room the hygge winter glow I was searching for. It will likely do the same for your space!

LINGERING GARLANDS

When January comes around, I'm never quite ready to fully say goodbye to all of my holiday decorations, so I leave some of them up for a little bit longer. I love to leave some greenery out, which can be anything from garlands to little trees. This lets the smell of pine still linger in the air, allowing my home to feel super wintery. Alpine trees covered in twinkle lights like these ones add such a cozy touch to the bathroom, along with some tiny bottlebrush trees above the beam.

Snow Globe Platter

This DIY adds a special touch of warmth to any room. It's super simple and can be an activity done with kids. You can use the platter in your bathroom to store toiletries on top of, or even put it on your kitchen counter to cover with treats. There are so many different ways to use it, which is part of the charm. The string lights are optional, but add a nice glowing touch during the darker days.

You'll need:

Glass bubble ball bowl

Faux snow

Tiny bottlebrush trees

Small deer figurines

Battery-powered string lights

Hot glue gun

Flat wooden plate

1. Fill the glass ball bowl about one-third of the way up with the faux snow.

2. Add the trees, deer, and string lights inside the bowl, arranged to your liking. Be sure the battery pack to the lights is left outside of the glass, so you can turn it on and off.

3. Hot glue the plate to the top of the bubble ball bowl to secure it in place.

LEAN INTO GREEN

In my Long Beach home, I also like to lean into the theme of winter greenery during the cold months at the start of the year. I swap out my holiday towels in the bathroom for pine tree towels. The pops of green help give the space a calm, serene vibe. I love to fill up a glass container with pine tree bath bombs for easily accessible use whenever I'm seeking a hot soak to warm up my chilled bones, but it also perfectly doubles as fun décor. I also like to cut out and hang some white paper trees above my bath for an extra wintery touch.

EVERGREEN ENTRYWAY

After the holidays die down, I try to remove all the reds and Christmas lights in my entryway at my Long Beach home, but I leave remnants of garlands, bottlebrush trees, and of course, a nod to our A-frame! During the colder months, I find having some baskets to use as catch-alls for beanies, scarves, and gloves is an easy way to keep my family organized. It also looks nice and reduces the feeling of clutter by the front door. I enjoy keeping an evergreen-scented candle on my entryway table so when guests come over, they walk into a calm space that feels warm and cozy, in contrast to the usually windy and cold outdoors. It also makes my home smell great!

FEBRUARY

I always congratulate myself when I make it to February. Getting started with a new year is often challenging, so once February rolls around, it feels like I'm no longer in the thick of adjusting. It helps that the arrival of this month also means we're almost halfway through winter. Not to rush the winter months away (since I am notoriously a cold-weather lover), but February always does feel like I'm in a better state of acceptance and settling into the year nicely. New routines are formed, resolutions are either being followed through with, or being thrown into the wind. The days are starting to pass a bit quicker than the snail's pace of early January, and there's a bit more light in the evenings as the days slowly grow longer. It's also the month of love—for me both because of Valentine's Day and because of my wedding anniversary, which falls right after the notorious day, on February 15th.

As I get older, I'm not as invested in focusing just on this one day to share and show love, since I ultimately believe we should be loving one another more freely every day, but the side of me that enjoys a holiday theme still leans into all the Valentine's décor the universe has to offer. From February 1st through the 14th, my entire world turns heart-themed. Sweaters covered in hearts, strawberries cut into hearts for my kids, heart-shaped pancakes, and heart-shaped pizzas. You name it, and I probably own it or have baked it into a heart shape during February. It's a fun challenge, even if you're the kind of person who wears black on the 14th and wakes up every year on this day with zero expectations. So whether you're a down-with-love kind of person, a hopeless romantic, or somewhere in between, the upbeat nature of seasonal décor that's entirely focused on love is a nice change of pace to bring some joy into what is otherwise a cold, wet, wintery month.

For that very reason, having a landing place for coats and snowy boots is so important during the wetter months, especially February which is often the snowiest month upstate. I try to marry function with aesthetics by adding in some cute baskets to catch beanies and scarves and to fill with pine cones for texture. I antiqued this snowy scene from a local shop, and I just love how pretty it looks on this ledge, with the world covered in white right outside reflecting a similar scene.

SCANDINAVIAN INSPIRED

A clean, neutral, Scandinavian-inspired dining space for February is functional, but still has enough touches of décor to make it feel warm and inviting. This aesthetic also allows you to add in holiday-focused pieces as well. I like to add a candlestick and a heart-shaped candle onto a tree-stump charger at the center of the table. Adding a fur shag onto a chair always makes a space feel a bit more lived-in.

ROMANTICIZE YOUR KITCHEN

A really simple way to add some festive Valentine's Day touches around the kitchen is to swap out any mugs on display and add some garland. I adore the simple design of these heart mugs. They add a hint of love to the space in an understated way. I also swap out my oven mitt and add a candle to bring some light in for those slow mornings when I make breakfast at home. I created this DIY woodland garland to hang on the open shelf which brings a bit of whimsy and romance into the space. The firefly lights do a great job of illuminating this dark corner too.

DIY

Paper Hearts

If you're craving a small, colorful change for Valentine's Day, this paper heart garland can make a big difference! It adds a lovely pop of reds and pinks and helps create interest in a spot that might otherwise be ignored.

You'll need:

Scissors

Red, pink, and white construction paper

Scoring stylus

Clear fishing line

Small plastic Command Hooks with light clips

1. Cut out dozens of hearts in all three colors. You can create a heart template and then trace it so you have hearts of uniform size.

2. Use the scoring stylus to poke pin-sized holes into the top of each heart.

3. String the clear fishing line through each hole, and tie a knot around each one as you go to keep it in place. Add as many hearts as you'd like to the different threads to reach the length you desire.

4. The garlands can be hung in windows, on walls, in doorways, or elsewhere using small Command Hooks at the top of each strand and knotting the garland to keep it in place. I created five threads to fill the width of the window and would suggest making this many, or more for a fuller look.

Woodland Garland

I'm not a huge fan of the color pink, so I like to keep some of my Valentine's Day décor natural and earthy. I love the woodsy feeling of these hearts, especially since they stay true to the general color scheme I feel comfortable displaying in my home.

You'll need:

Brown twig garland

Gold wire

Twine

1. Cut the garland so you can easily shape it into a heart.

2. Bend the garland into a heart shape, and wrap gold wire around it to hold it together. Use the gold wire to twist both ends of the twine together.

3. Use the gold wire to attach the hearts together in a row.

4. Tie a piece of twine to each end to hang up the garland.

Fluffy Focaccia

If you're interested in winter baking, but bread feels intimidating, a focaccia is an easy place to start! Personally, I like it when baking feels like decorating in some way, so I made this standard focaccia recipe my own by adding a cute little mushroom design onto the top.

SERVES: 4–6
TIME: 2 hours, plus ~10 hours resting time

Ingredients:
¼oz envelope active dry yeast
2 tsp honey
5 cups (700g) all-purpose flour
1 tbsp kosher salt
6 tbsp extra-virgin olive oil, divided,
  plus more for coating hands
4 tbsp unsalted butter
1-2 red/orange peppers
1 onion
2-4 cloves garlic, for garnish
Fresh rosemary, for garnish
Fresh thyme, for garnish
Flaky sea salt
Sesame seeds, for garnish, if desired

1. In a medium bowl, whisk together the dry yeast, honey, and 2½ cups lukewarm water. Let sit for 5 minutes.

2. Add the flour and kosher salt, and mix with a spatula until a lumpy, yet well-combined dough forms.

3. In a separate medium bowl, pour in 4 tablespoons of the olive oil. Transfer the dough into the olive oil in this bowl, and cover with plastic wrap. Let rest until the dough has doubled in size, at least 8 hours and up to 1 day.

4. Using a fork in each hand, gather the edges of the dough and lift them up and over to bring them into the center of the bowl. Repeat this process to deflate the dough while forming it into a rough ball.

5. Butter a square baking dish. Pour 1 tablespoon of the olive oil into the center of the dish. Transfer the dough to the prepared dish, and pour any leftover oil on top. Let the dough rise for another 1½ hours to 4 hours, until it once again doubles in size.

6. Preheat the oven to 450°F (232°C).

7. Lightly oil your hands, and dimple the focaccia all over with your fingers.

8. Cut into the peppers and remove the seeds. Cut the peppers into shapes that resemble the tops of mushrooms, and cut the onions into small ½-inch rectangles for the mushroom stems.

9. Add the peppers, onion, garlic, rosemary, and thyme on top of the focaccia in the pattern of a few mushrooms, and drizzle all over with the remaining oil before baking. Sprinkle on the flaky sea salt.

10. Place the focaccia in the oven on the middle rack, and bake for 20 to 30 minutes or until it's puffed and golden brown. Sprinkle on sesame seeds once removed from the oven for another extra touch, if desired.

As winter fades into spring, the snow melts and the world fills up with more color again.
I never complain seeing it go, but I always look back on the mornings when I could open my blinds to see the world blanketed in white with warmth in my heart.

SPRING

While I live for a cool, crisp morning in the fall or a winter morning where I wake up to a world covered in white, I'd be lying if I said I don't cringe when I still have to put on my winter jacket and gloves once March hits. By the time this month comes around, I wake up every morning and check the temperature. If it's still below 50°F (10°C), I quickly find myself groaning.

The arrival of spring, when it finally comes, is such a relief—it's knowing that sunnier days are ahead, it's getting to be outside more, and it's seeing the world in full bloom once again. There are two big days I look forward to most in spring—the first time I can wear shorts, and the day when it's warm enough outside to make my first iced coffee of the season.

I remember these days vividly each year—looking down at my pasty legs and thinking how foreign they look to me. As I cross my legs, it's kind of a weird sensation to not have a thick layer of jeans or fabric in between them anymore. It's always a welcome development when I wake up to walk my dog Claude and realize the air outside is warm enough for me to add ice to my morning coffee. These are just two of the signs in my life that make me recognize spring is starting.

Once I make these daily routine shifts, it marks a new beginning for me—the beginning of warmer, longer days. I may be ready to say goodbye to them once the start of fall approaches, but when they first arrive, I am so very ready to say hello to them as winter ends.

Seeing the forsythia bloom around our property adds such a beautiful contrast to the exterior orange color of our home. I always use the yellows and pinks outside as inspiration for the color scheme of the décor inside.

MARCH

Do you ever wake up in the morning, look around at your space, and think, "I need to change everything?" This is what March is like for me. I generally begin March with some leftover greenery still sprinkled around my house from Christmas, keeping in the theme of winter vibes, but once March 1st hits, I immediately feel the need for it all to be gone.

Technically, spring doesn't officially come until toward the end of the month, but as the temperatures warm up, my décor always follows suit by becoming lighter and brighter.

Deep greens shift into pastel oranges and pinks. Heavy blankets are swapped for linens and cottons. And as the flowers slowly begin to bloom outside, I find ways to bring them inside as well. I usually prefer to live within a color scheme of warm hues: oranges, yellows, and browns, but when early spring comes around, all my typical color preferences get tossed away. I absolutely need to be surrounded by life, and brighter colors!

If you're ready for warmer days ahead, but they haven't quite shown up outside your door yet, one of my best kept secrets is to fake it. Something I love to change early on, right at the cusp of a new season are rugs and throw pillows. It's something easy to do that completely transforms the colors in your space. In March, I swap out my winter rug for something lighter and brighter that brings more color into my home. I choose to keep some thicker blankets and pillows mixed in for cooler nights when I can't quite heat my toes up. This makes March feel like a transitional month, which it is!

Flower Arch

I like to look at my front door as a way to share my décor with my neighborhood (whether they ask for it or not). When you live in a small town, or even in a big city where you walk a lot, you tend to notice when your neighbors change things. If my neighbor paints their door, or plants some new flowers for the season, I see it and it brings me joy. I also see the time and effort they spent on it. Whenever I'm outside, I find I connect with my neighbors most as they walk by and ask me what I'm working on. Installing a floral arch above my doorway was a nice way to spend half a day, chatting with neighbors, listening to the birds chirping, and transforming the front of the A-frame. This flower arch really tied in nicely to all the flowers and trees blooming around it!

You'll need:

Scissors

Plastic chicken wire

Clear outdoor removable hooks

Faux garland

Green gardening wire

Faux flowers

1. Cut the chicken wire into 3 premeasured pieces—one for above the door, and two for either side of the door.

2. Hold up the chicken wire, and get an idea of where to place the clear removable hooks that will attach the chicken wire to the wall.

3. Peel off the backs of the removable hooks and attach them to the home.

4. Hang the chicken wire and make sure it is secure on the hooks.

5. Attach the faux garland with the gardening wire to the chicken wire, which should add fullness to the arch. Make sure there is good coverage, but not so much coverage that the flowers won't fit.

6. Begin to add faux flowers throughout, attaching with the gardening wire and filling in any gaps. Try to make the garland look more blended together and less like garland.

7. Trim the chicken wire at any spots where it obviously shows.

POPS OF COLOR

Changing out the pillows is one of the quickest ways I transform my living room. I added this hook sunshine pillow from the local shop Maverick Road (located in Woodstock, New York), along with a splash of floral vibes from an additional retro-inspired pillow.

Adding spring colors with flowers is another simple way to take a living room into the next season. I love to find pastel flowers at my local market and display them on the side tables to warm up the space.

I enjoy seasonally changing out my coffee table candy dishes too—this time including some pastel-colored mints that nicely compliment the pillow color!

St Patrick's Day

#1 CLOVER BALLOON WALL

St Patrick's Day is pretty huge in Long Beach since
a majority of the residents are Irish, including my
Uncle Pat who lives around the block. Before going
out for some Irish cocktails at the local bars, it's fun
to dress up in green and take some photos—so adding
a photo wall is one of my favorite DIYs! It adds so
much to photos with friends (or your kids) before
heading out, and takes under ten minutes to install!

#2 GREEN CANDY JARS

During the week St. Patrick's Day falls, I love to
peruse the candy aisle at the supermarket and pick
up some green candies to display in my entryway. I
picked up these green coins for an extra pop of color!
A trick I love to use for candy jars is filling the largest
jar with a medium sized jar flipped upside down so
you need less candy to fill it up. It gives the
appearance of a much fuller jar.

LONG BEACH
FRONT DOOR

A few years back, my son Hudson was wearing these incredible mustard-yellow overalls, and I decided to go to a paint store and color match his outfit to paint our front door the same color. Surprisingly, the mustard-yellow color is shockingly adaptable from season to season. It's such a fun shade to work with decorating around! I generally don't swap out my doormat or front patio décor until later in spring when I know the weather has officially made a turn for the better. I love to add some jute lanterns to illuminate warmer nights and a green wreath with an airy spring feeling to it. In late spring, I also add some plants that I look forward to watering every morning. I usually set my front patio up, and then make small décor changes with mat and flower swaps to refresh the space month to month.

APRIL

There is only one special week the entire year when I can look out of my son's upstairs window in Long Beach and see the cherry blossoms blooming on the tree outside. During that same week, 2½ hours away, the gorgeous pink tree in front of the A-frame also blooms, and the streets surrounding our home are lined with bright yellow forsythia. Ironically, half of the trees are still leafless, but simultaneously the other half shine so bright with blooming flowers. It makes my eyes light up. The saying goes that April showers bring May flowers, but in my universe, all the best flowers show their pretty little faces in April. They slink their way into my memories—year after year, this is the week I always remember with such clarity.

From seeing my older son play in what was once his playroom, with the cherry blossoms peeking in through the window, to putting my newborn down for a nap in the same room after we converted it to a nursery, the vibrant cherry blossoms fade away as I pull the blackout shades down. I remember Charlie at one month past one, just learning to stand in that same crib as the blooms flourished—the same year we were able to see them for the first time at the A-frame. April is a special month.

Pastel Painted Stripes

By April, I've brought color into my home in all the simple ways that can brighten up the space. It's at this point that I decide to pull out all the stops and get my hands dirty. This usually involves painting a wall or a door, and wow, does a fresh coat of paint really transform the space—and for an affordable price too! This wall behind our dining room table at the A-frame is the perfect example of a focal wall that feels small enough to tackle painting in a few hours, so I decided to add some pastel stripes to it. It was a time-consuming process, but in the end, it came out so vibrant! I used Benjamin Moore AURA Interior Paint in the shades Sun Blossom 149 and Marblehead Gold HC-11, but you can use any two colors you like.

You'll need:
Painter's tape
Laser level
Paint brushes
Two paint colors of your choice

1. Tape 12-inch thick stripes on your wall using the laser level to make sure they are straight and don't look wonky.

2. Paint two coats on the first stripes (alternating every other stripe), and let them dry.

3. Once the first color of stripes is dry, pull the tape off and then tape over the previously painted stripes to paint the next color.

4. Again, paint two coats for these stripes and let them dry. Pull off the tape when totally dry, and touch up any spots as necessary with a smaller brush.

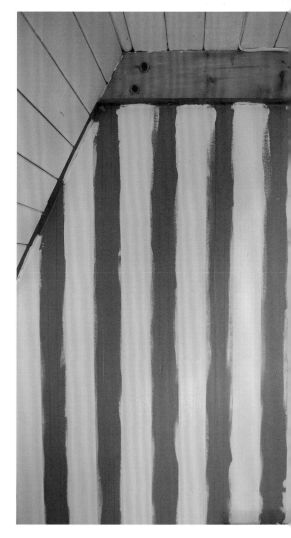

SPRING GLASSWARE

I have a weak spot for vintage glassware. And it's so easy to find them in almost every antique shop across Upstate New York. Shopping for glassware is particularly appealing in the spring since it's when all the vintage lemon pitchers come out! This yellow, lemon-shaped pitcher is vintage gold, and it looks so cute on my open shelf next to some floral bows and mugs.

These pink antique mugs add just the right hint of pink as I am not much of a pink-lover usually. Small swaps like these change the entire feeling of our kitchen from a cozy and wintery haven to a sunshine-filled spot to make morning coffee and eggs.

EASTER TABLESCAPING

If you're hosting Easter, or you just enjoy dressing up your table, consider adding a floral runner and some floral textures to the dining room table in April. Antique stores are a great place to start for inspiration. I found these adorable orange salt and pepper shakers at a local shop in Tannersville, New York. I love to play with textures and patterns, so I paired jute chargers with striped reusable napkins to bring some life to this table setting.

Board & Batten

When April rolls around, I return to my endless list of larger DIY projects—the ones that require me to use power tools and cut wood outside—that I avoid doing in the dead of winter. I'd been wanting to install a board and batten entryway wall in this space, and as the weather warmed up, it finally felt like time. The board and batten moment is so nice for seasonal décor swaps. For spring, I added some dried-out florals and a pops of yellow with a candle and a book.

You'll need:	Tools needed:
1in × 2in × 8ft pieces of wood, as many as needed	Circular saw or miter saw
¼in × 2in piece of wood	Ryobi brad nailer
Paint, color of your choice	Level

1. Start by painting the wall. I used Benjamin Moore Tricorn Black paint, but you can pick any color you like. Use a minimum of two coats.

2. Measure the length you'd like to cut your battens down to, and trim the 1 in × 2 in × 8 ft pieces of wood with the saw as necessary to achieve this length.

3. Cut one batten into a shorter, middle spacer so you can use it to help achieve the same distance between each vertical batten that is attached to the wall.

4. One by one, attach the trimmed battens to the wall with the brad nailer, using the spacer to ensure equal distance between each. Check the level of each piece as you go.

5. Once all the battens are securely attached, add the ledge shelf on top. Attach it using the brad nailer, and paint the newly installed pieces!

PAINTING FLOWERS

A very simple way to add some spring touches to your space is to paint an entryway mirror.
Acrylic paint dries quickly and comes off easily. I added these pastel flowers to my entryway
mirror to welcome the new season.

Swapping out white candles for pastel-colored ones can instantly transform the feeling of a space.

MAY

During the first week of May, I take my first bike ride of the year in shorts and a t-shirt. I send Mother's Day flowers and walk with my kids to school after months of driving them. I work on projects like painting my best friend's driveway in a tank top, have my first beach day, and usually experience my first day of the year feeling like the temperature outside is hot. May, while still spring, is the segue into summer. It's when the outdoors become my home and the indoors become only a brief spot to eat my meals, take my baths, and sleep at night. This is the month when I can stop checking the weather forecast before getting dressed each morning and know with certainty that it will be warm enough to show some skin. It's when I officially fold up my favorite sweaters for later in the year and place my Vans and sandals in a more accessible place for daily wear. In May, my home is filled with fresh flowers, colors, and lots of sunscreen for easy grabbing whenever we head outside.

DIY

Hanging Flowers

Some spaces don't need much to feel beautiful—and my upstairs bedroom at the A-frame is one of those spaces. The large windows paired with the striking angles that the beams create causes the room to require very little color and décor. For May, as more flowers bloom outside, I like to bring some of that color into my space. I chose faux flowers in a warm rainbow color scheme, with pops of oranges, yellows, and pinks. These hanging flowers add such a nice amount of color, while not making the space feel too bright or cluttered. The installation only takes about 30 minutes, and is very easy to take down.

You'll need:

Scissors

Clear fishing line

Faux flowers

Gorilla double sided tape

1. Cut the fishing line to various lengths so the flowers hang at different heights.

2. Attach the flowers to the fishing line by either tying the line around the base of the flower or by poking a hole through the fabric and weaving it through.

3. Tape the end of the fishing line up to the ceiling.

4. Stagger the flowers at different heights as you hang them, which will help the space have a more natural and whimsical feeling. Some strands can have just a single flower while others can have up to three.

WARMING UP
THE BATHROOM

One of the simplest and most effective seasonal swaps to lighten and brighten a bathroom is to change the color of the bath mat to something unexpected. I designed the A-frame bathroom with a neutral color palette in mind—beiges, greens, and a lot of bright whites. Adding a pop of pink for May, along with some fresh florals, completely changes the feeling of the room. The color of the pink runner against the dark green tile is an unexpected contrast that really brings the warm weather and the blooms inside.

BRIGHT PATTERNS & BOLD TONES

Adding a throw blanket that shows off bright patterns and bold tones onto the bed is a simple way to add more color into your space. I paired this floral blanket with some fresh flowers on the nightstand, which helps make the room feel warm and springy.

Sparkling Lavender Lemon Cocktail

This cocktail is for all the prosecco lovers out there—like me! It's light, airy, and tastes quite literally like spring. First, you'll make a lavender simple syrup to use as a mixer, then you'll add it to some bubbly prosecco.

SERVES: 2–4 // **TIME:** 2½ hours

Ingredients:
1 cup (237 ml) water
3 tbsp food-grade dried lavender flowers
2 cups (480g) sugar
2–4 lemons
1 (750 ml) bottle of prosecco
Lavender sprigs, for garnish

1. In a medium-sized pot, combine the water with the dried lavender flowers and bring to a boil.

2. Once boiling, add the sugar and cook until fully dissolved.

3. Turn down the heat, and let simmer on low for 15 minutes.

4. Remove the mixture from the heat and let steep for up to 1 hour. Strain out the lavender. Store in the fridge, and let chill for a minimum of 1 hour.

5. Add 1 tablespoon of the chilled lavender simple syrup you've made to each glass.

6. Cut one lemon in half, and squeeze one-half into each glass. Cut the other lemon into thin wedges to use for garnish.

7. Add prosecco into each glass, filling it up toward the top.

8. Garnish each glass with a sprig of lavender and a lemon slice. Cheers!

SPRING CLOSET

I like to view my closet and my clothing as an extension of my seasonal décor. Usually, if I'm decorating in a certain color scheme, you'll be able to walk into my closet and find that same color scheme in what I'm wearing. (What can I say? I'm predictable.) My general rule is if I wake up for a full week and the weather is 70°F (21°C) and warmer, then it's time for my closet to get swapped out.

The biggest swap happens with my other babies—my shoes. I have a large collection of vintage boots for fall and winter that I move out of reach, and I pull out all my Vans, Converse, sandals, white sneakers, and generally less fashion-forward, but more wearable shoes. As the bike rides become more frequent, the trendy boots become more infrequent. I am a little less put together in the summer, but I'm totally okay with that. My summer dresses, chambrays, and short-sleeve shirts become more front and center, with bright colors and 70s-inspired floral patterns making their way to the more accessible parts of my closet.

Mother's Day

If there's one thing most of my mom friends enjoy, it's wine. Wine night, wine brunch, just wine of any kind! So there's no better surprise on Mother's Day than a beautiful DIY ice mold (accompanying a brunch, of course). This mold never fails to delight. It can be filled with anything from faux flowers, fruit, or even a favorite candy. It is also reusable, and can be refilled as many times, or as many Mother's Days, as you like!

You'll need:

Plastic ice mold

Faux flowers

Freezer

1. Fill the plastic ice mold with faux flowers in the pattern of your choice.

2. Add water to the fill line.

3. Place in the freezer overnight.

4. Pull the ice mold out of the freezer about an hour before use, and run some room temperature water into the center of the mold to help remove the frozen ice from the plastic.

5. Place your chosen bottle of wine into the center of the mold and place it on display for all the moms to enjoy!

The previous owner of the A-frame planted beautiful perennials around the property, and when the daffodils bloom, it's the very first sign that spring has arrived at our home.

SUMMER

During my childhood, my parents always made sure we spent a ton of time together as a family over the summer. Sleepaway camp was a no-go, as were trips with friends. Every year we made the 22-hour drive from New York to Florida, where I was squished together in the backseat of our SUV with a brother on either side of me. We headed to the sunshine state to spend the summer together with cousins, aunts, and uncles. On the way, I often elbowed my brothers to get off me as they fell asleep, their heads slowly drooping onto my shoulders, their toys crowding the space where my feet should have been able to touch the floor. One year, we stopped at South of the Border and laughed about what a letdown it was. Another year we stopped at Kings Dominion in Virginia to ride roller coasters together for the first time. Regardless of our pit stops along the drive, we'd always bicker and fight, but we'd laugh, too, staying up late to share stories from summers prior.

I think back on those summers differently as a mom now. At the time, I couldn't wait for them to end, but now, I yearn for them, longing for the feeling of open days, time melting together, and yes, even the boredom. This is the key word I like to plan all my summers around these days—boredom. I love to spend summer afternoons full of nothingness with my sons, where we can be together. As long as it's just us, somewhere outside, probably at the beach making sandcastles, I know they'll recall these memories fondly.

Summer in Upstate New York is so lush. The trees in our driveway fill in, and our property suddenly feels more private as it bursts with greenery. The creek down the street has a swimming hole where you can take a dip surrounded by the woods.

JUNE

There's something invigorating about beginnings and the unknowns that come along with them—knowing who you are at the start, and wondering who you will be at the end. At the beginning of summer, you can look at your calendar and see weeks and weeks of emptiness ahead, just waiting to be filled with ice cream that always melts quicker than you can eat it and nights spent underneath café lights in the backyard. June is when it all begins. It's when your summer tan is just starting and the hot days and later sunsets feel brand new. It's when you pick up your seasonal flowers and find your new summertime routines—the ones that will define your slower living for the next three months. I love the mystery of what lies ahead each summer, and I always welcome the more casual pace of life that this month beckons with open arms.

In June, as the flowers outside begin to morph into lush greenery, I slowly begin to reflect this in my décor. I love to simplify the bright, pastel colors of spring and opt for a color scheme that is a bit more neutral. I like playing up pops of greens by picking up vinca vines (easy to keep alive if you are a notorious plant killer like me) and mixing them in with some faux greenery. I enjoy this combination for the sake of keeping it alive and green even while traveling during the summer months. I also love to clip branches off my trees outside and place them around my space in thrifted vases and mason jars. Bringing plants inside really livens up the space and also adds color to the airiness of a neutral color scheme. My color scheme transforms from pops of pastels and an overflow of florals to crisp whites paired with pops of green and natural textures mixed in.

Since I have the privilege of having screens on my doors and windows, I love to crack them open for some fresh air in the early mornings and late afternoons during June when the weather is usually not scorching hot. I love to see the overwhelming greenery outside the A-frame and watch the light change throughout the day.

POPS OF GREEN

My days in June usually begin with a routine of waking up, making my morning coffee, and watering my plants. I love to fill my space with plenty of plants during the bright summery months, mixing various neutral-colored pots with antique paintings and floral-scented candles. Neutral hues with pops of green is my go-to color scheme as summer starts. I keep the table set with jute chargers, bowls of fruit, and thrifted napkins that have strawberries needlepointed onto them. Fruit is always in an easy-to-grab place, and it doubles as part of the décor!

Father's Day

Finding wrapping paper that feels right can be difficult. If you're looking for a way to include your kids in a Father's Day gift without actually letting them pick out the gift (because that usually doesn't go over so well), creating DIY wrapping paper can be a fun idea! You can choose to draw the pattern yourself, or allow the kids to get involved. I found a cute #1 Dad ribbon and felt inspired to paint it onto my wrapping paper. The finished product looks handmade in the best way possible, and it feels extra special to hand a gift covered in this paper to a well-deserving dad!

You'll need:

Pencil

Wrapping paper roll, plain brown is preferred

Paint brushes

Acrylic paint, colors of your choice

1. Outline a pattern in pencil on plain wrapping paper to ensure the design is spaced evenly. Erase any errors that may occur.

2. Once you are happy with your drawings and the spacing, paint the designs onto the wrapping paper using acrylic paint.

3. Let the paint dry for a few hours, then use the finished paper to wrap your Father's Day gifts.

Swapping out the shower curtain for something more colorful and adding some green plants above the tub can really liven up the bathroom for summer.

NEUTRALS & PLANTS

One of the easiest changes I make to bring the feeling of June into my kitchen is swapping out the rug in front of the sink. I found this green-toned floral rug from Anthropologie, and it pairs perfectly with the greenery all around my kitchen. The vinca vines hanging from my open shelving and the fresh eucalyptus in the vase next to my sink make my kitchen feel cohesive next to the dining room. I swap out my mugs for ones that look like the naked bodies of women with different skin tones, which showcases my desire to be less clothed during the warmer months. I always feel freer in how I dress during summer, and freer in how I live my days. June is when I have a less-packed schedule, more free time to spend spontaneously outdoors, and the chance to tend to projects, plants, and friends!

LONGER DAYS, BRIGHTER BATHROOMS

Throughout June, I love to play up how bright our bathrooms feel. Since the sun sets later and later, the light that comes pouring in from the window behind the soaker tub seems to linger all day. Some baby's breath flowers make the space feel fresh, and I pull out my summer perfume to put on display. It's a scent that captures the salty air, and warm, sticky summer nights.

In the boys' bathroom, I change the shower curtain to a beautiful sepia-gold color and pair it with a yellow-orange bath mat to bring those bright, bold hues of summer days inside for bath time.

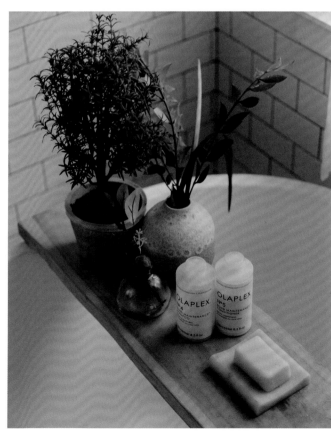

LEMONADE STAND

Nothing screams summer for kids like a lemonade stand. I remember often dreaming of running my own as a kid, but I lived on a cul-de-sac where cars rarely drove by and there were absolutely zero walkers about since my street growing up didn't even have sidewalks. Luckily for my kids, we live on the main street that leads down to the beach—the ideal spot for running a summer lemonade stand. I had some scrap wood lying around, so I decided to build this stand over a weekend, being sure to paint it with bold yellow and white stripes to get our neighbors' attention as they walked past.

JULY

When I was young, I remember feeling sad about not being able to celebrate my July birthday during the school year. I was one of the summer babies who was grouped together with the other kids who had birthdays in June, July, and August at the big end-of-year summer birthday celebration where there was one cake for 10 kids' birthdays. After we ate our cake and said goodbye, we dispersed for the summer, off to celebrate our birthdays on our own time, in our own little bubbles. I'd usually have a family party, where I was surrounded by my cousins, brothers, aunts and uncles, hundreds of miles away in Florida from all my friends. I always felt like I was missing out by never having my best friend at my side while we sang happy birthday.

Now, as an adult, I love being a summer baby. When July rolls around, it means it's my birthday month and it's summer at the same time! For me, July means beach days, barbeques, fireworks, and bonfires. Aside from being the month I was born, July is also the month that's right in the very thick of summer. This is the month when all my warm-weather routines that are so engrained in me can come to the surface. My beach prep becomes second nature: my cooler is always on the kitchen counter waiting to be packed, and my beach chairs and toys wait in our beach cart in the garage. The days are long, the weekends are far shorter than I'd like them to be, and the time I spend enjoying sunsets and fresh pizza are the memories I know I'll revisit all year long.

SEASONAL CLOTHING
SECONDING AS DÉCOR

I love to highlight summer vibes in the entryway by adding some fresh hydrangeas and displaying
sunglasses in wicker baskets to easily grab on the way out for sunny days. I often hang up a denim shirt to
have a nice summer texture present. It's also perfect to have easily accessible for any chilly summer nights
when a second layer is needed.

BRINGING GREENERY INSIDE

In July, every direction I look outside my window is blooming and green. This feeling is what finally pushed me to paint an accent wall behind my bed at the A-frame. Inspired by green, I chose the Sherwin Williams color Evergreen Fog. It only took two coats of paint, and the outcome looks so beautiful against the lush green that peeks in through the triangle window. The bedroom was transformed from white with pops of pastel colors during the spring months to a calm, tranquil, green oasis. The second I open my eyes each summer morning I see the greenery outside coming in through our skylight, and it feels so very much like July! If you're looking to paint an accent wall in your space, just know it's an affordable and quick way to transform a room into something new.

GAZEBO PAINT REFRESH

One of my main projects for July was to refresh our gazebo and get her ready for the upcoming fall season! Since the A-frame had been painted the year prior, the gazebo was due for a fresh coat. Can't you just see it with some pumpkins on the shelves in a few months? For now though, it looks so cute on a late July afternoon with the string lights and some white flowers decorating the sides.

Trellis

If you have an outdoor wall space that feels plain, or forgotten, adding a DIY faux trellis is a perfect way to bring the space back to life for the summer season. I love this seating area on our front patio, but felt like it needed some greenery, so I went to work!

You'll need:

Outdoor Command Hooks

Floral wire

Grapevines

Faux ivy garland

Faux olive garland

1. Decide how tall and wide the trellis will be, and how much space will be between each string. Once the measurements are decided, stick outdoor Command Hooks evenly across the top, bottom, and sides of where you'd like the trellis to go.

2. Grab the floral wire and begin to string it through the Command Hooks at a diagonal to create the desired diamond shape. Skip every other hook so that the floral wire is placed diagonally.

3. Once all the floral wire is hung, attach the grapevines. Then layer on the faux ivy garland and a tiny bit of the faux olive garland on top.

The goal is to make it look as natural and realistic as possible, so imperfections are totally fine. You don't have to get too caught up in every piece lining up exactly. From a distance, I do think this trellis translates as realistic, and it adds such a warm touch. This became the perfect spot to have some wine with Matt in the late afternoons.

Fire Pit

When we bought the A-frame, one of the first projects on my list was a better fire pit that was centered with the house. Since the old one was uncomfortably close to the trees, I knew moving it over a few feet to the center of the yard would make a big difference. July is the perfect month to tackle something like this since there are so many hours of daylight to work outside. This DIY took me a total of five days from beginning to end, so be sure to pace yourself!

You'll need:

Metal stake

Measuring tape

String, yarn, or twine

White spray paint

Shovel

Level

Marble chips (35 bags for a 10-foot circle)

Rake

Metal fire ring

Quick drying mortar

Bucket (for mortar)

7in x 3.5in gray paver stones

1. Push a stake into the ground at the center of where your pit will be. Make sure the area is flat and level. For a pit with a 10-foot circumference, tie a 5-foot piece of string around a spray paint can and tie the other end of the string to the stake. Pull the string taught, and spray the outline of the pit by moving the spray paint can around the perimeter.

2. Dig out the area inside the spray-painted circle until it is 5 inches deep and level.

3. Add the marble chips by dumping them into the dug-out hole. Use a rake to move them around and level them out.

4. Place a metal fire ring in the center of the circle, and lay the paver stones around it, stone by stone. Use quick-drying mortar to cement the stones together. You can mix it up as you work, making small batches so it won't dry up too quickly. Four or five layers of stones are ideal to surround the ring.

5. Mortar stones around the edge of the fire pit circle by placing mortar along the border of the circle and carefully laying the paver stones one by one. Add some chairs and some wood, and you'll be enjoying a cozy summer bonfire in no time!

Firewood Storage

Once the fire pit was built, I knew I wanted to build a place to store our firewood. Then the idea came to me to create a mini version of the A-frame! This was a fairly easy build, and it looks so charming next to our home.

You'll need:	Tools needed:
Four 2 × 4s	Miter saw
3in wood screws	Power drill
1 sheet of plywood	Electric sander
2 cinder blocks	
Wood stain	

1. Use the miter saw to cut the ends of four pieces of 2x4s. After these are cut, they should fit together to create two triangular A-frame shapes that line up along the mitered edges. Drill two of the 2 × 4s together to create the first frame, and then repeat for the second frame.

2. Select the depth you want your wood-holder to be, and then cut two bottom 2 × 4 supports and one top support to attach the two frames together. The two bottom supports will fasten on the inside of the A-frame shapes and the top support will fasten at the top of the interior, screwed in an inch below the peak of the A-frame. Place the structure into the cinder blocks for support.

3. Cut the plywood to size, and drill the roof onto the frame on both sides.

4. Sand and stain the entire structure and paint the cinder blocks if desired.

AUGUST

August is a controversial month according to the internet. There's always a debate during this month about how soon is too soon to say fall is "just around the corner." A great divide appears between summer-lovers who don't want their summers to slip away, and fall-fanatics who are salivating to put their pumpkins out and reach for their pumpkin spice lattes on August 23rd, when they usually become available. The core problem is that retailers made the judgment call years ago and decided that August is indeed a fair month to stock fall décor. You may sweat your way from your air-conditioned car into the local Michaels and be stunned to find maple leaf garland and faux pumpkins in mid-August as your cheeks are flushed and the back of your neck is covered in sweat. But in my mind, if the stores are selling it, then it's fair game. And even though I live steps from the beach, by the end of August, my home has hints of fall all around. Maybe it's simply a pumpkin-scented candle, or maybe I'll paint my front door a shade of orange to get ready for the new, over-the-top fall décor that's coming soon.

So, while August does lie fully within the summer season, in my home, it is an outlier, and I like to view it more as prefall, rather than summer's end. Most of the time, the anticipation of something great is even better than the something great itself, and August is just that. It is knowing that the basic fall-lovers (like myself) will be in all their fall glory very, very soon—and sometimes knowing that is even better than standing amongst the foliage drinking a PSL.

A BEDROOM
READY FOR FALL

During the early months of summer, my home
generally feels light and airy, with tons of vibrant
plant life and pops of green against a neutral
backdrop. But as August rolls around, before I pull
out my pumpkins and plaids (I know, fall technically
starts late-September), I begin the seasonal change
early by pulling out more warm colors and shifting
the color scheme throughout my home. I swap out
my duvet cover for a burnt-orange shade, giving my
bedroom a cozier feeling. It's a simple way to kick off
a seasonal shift without pulling out all the small
seasonal décor yet!

A KITCHEN IN SHADES OF ORANGE

One of my favorite things about color is how our interpretation of the meanings behind colors feel so endless. How I answer the question "What does the color orange mean to you?" is totally relative to the time and place at which you ask me.

During a seasonal shift, like in the month of August, I love to question those meanings and think about how to apply them to my décor. In early summer, when I see orange, I think of freshly squeezed citrus and long summer days, but come the end of August, I think more of foxes, pumpkins, the changing leaves coming soon, pumpkin pie, and everything autumnal. The color has not changed at all, only my perspective has. When styling my open shelves in August, I keep all of this in mind and try to marry the two seasonal interpretations I hold of orange into one location. I mix fox mugs with vintage orange pitchers and bowls of lemons and limes. For me, the melding of different ideas—all in the same color scheme—really captures the essence of the end of one season and the beginning of a new one.

FRESH AIR IN THE UPSTAIRS BATHROOM

If there's one easy way to make a bathroom space feel more like summer, it's as simple as adding some jute. Swapping out a bright pink runner for something jute instantly makes the space feel more airy and light. Letting some fresh air in throughout the day by cracking the doors and windows also helps make the space feel bright. I love to add a wreath with greenery to the door, as well as some fresh-potted greens on the side table and atop the toilet to bring some of the lushness of the outdoors inside.

Peel & Stick Wallpaper

The trick to using peel and stick wallpaper is to stick the sheet to the wall and worry about cutting the top and the bottom excess off later. The first time I applied wallpaper, I tried to precut everything on the floor, but I quickly realized that it's much easier to make your cuts on the wall. The first piece you stick on is the most important, because if it's not level, it will throw off the entire wall!

You'll need:

Wallpaper of your choice

Level

Flat plastic rectangle, to smooth wallpaper

Exacto knife

Ruler or straight edge

1. For the first piece of wallpaper, use a level to check that your edge is straight after you stick it onto the wall, then smooth it out.

2. After the first piece is level and securely on the wall, start at the top and line up the second piece so that the seams are not visible. Carefully stick and smooth the remainder of the second piece, making sure the seams line up the whole way down the wall.

3. Once your sheets are applied, cut the excess off at the top and the bottom using your exacto knife and ruler. Apply these steps for the entire wall.

The perfect summer night is grabbing a blanket for when the temperature drops after sunset and cozying up with some white wine and fresh pizza at the picnic table.

Margherita Pizza

During Summer 2020 in the middle of lockdown, we were living with my parents for a few months at their home in Martha's Vineyard. My dad had a pipe dream to build a pizza oven in his backyard, so we spent our open-ended days doing just that. He ordered the top dome already put together, and we built the base it would sit on out of cinder blocks and stones that weighed around a ton. It was the authentic kind of oven that requires you to burn a fire in it each night for a week before actual use so the oven can properly crack and settle.

We built a fire at dusk each night, picked up fresh and local ingredients from the farm around the block, and made homemade pizza dough. Once we were out of lockdown, we missed our authentic pizza nights, so we found a slice of these joyful memories in the Ooni Fyra pizza oven. It requires pellets to burn, and can cook a 12-inch pie in around 1 minute. It's been so nice to bring some of the nostalgia of that summer to our A-frame yard and cook pizzas for neighbors or friends who stop by. We've been using the same recipe for years, and it works like a charm.

1. In a medium-size bowl, mix together the yeast and warm water. Add in the salt and flour.

2. Knead the dough for 10 minutes until it feels firm and not sticky.

3. Cover the dough with plastic wrap and let it rise for 1½ to 2 hours at room temperature, or until the dough has doubled in size.

4. Punch down the dough to form it into a large ball, and cut it into 3 pieces, approximately 275 grams each. This will make 3 pies.

5. Let the separated dough balls rise while covered with plastic wrap for at least 1 hour.

6. In a small pot, mix the sauce ingredients together over medium-low heat for 3 to 5 minutes. Once heated, coat the spread-out dough with an even layer. Place the mozzarella cheese over the sauce and top with fresh basil.

7. Cook in a pizza wood-fired oven for 1 minute or in a standard oven at 425°F (218°C) for 20 to 25 minutes, or until the edges of the crust are golden brown.

MAKES: three 10" pies // **TIME:** 3 hours

Dough:

1 tsp active dry yeast

1¼ cups (300g) warm water

2 tsp salt

3½ cups (490g) Caputo 00 flour

Sauce:

28oz can of tomato passata

¼ tsp black pepper

½ tsp salt

1 tsp oregano

Toppings:

8oz high-moisture mozzarella cheese

Fresh basil, for garnish

The string lights we put up outline the triangle silhouette of the A-frame. They transform the home as we go from sunny days into dark nights, helping it glow in all its late-summer glory.

FALL

It was 1994, and my dad and I were walking down the foliage-lined streets of Lynbrook, Long Island, in my aunt's neighborhood during peak fall. We were carrying an empty shopping bag to collect leaves in. I told my dad I wanted to collect as many as I could to remember what fall felt like. This would be my last one, since we were moving to Florida in the spring. I was only seven years old, but I remember every feeling from that day—the crisp air, the adoration I felt for my dad (who, by the way, had very little understanding or empathy for how deeply my love of fall ran), and the yearning for a season I was living and breathing in so deeply that my heart hurt. I pressed the leaves we collected that day into a book called *The Laugh Book* that had a yellow hardcover. I still have it.

Every year after we moved to Florida, when October came around and I was still sweating in my tank top and shorts, I would yearn for the falls of New York. I'd feel like I was missing out, missing the beautiful sights of fall colors and the feeling that our beautiful planet has so much to offer us. Sure, I lived by a beach and I never had to bundle up in tights and boots, but to me, it felt like a huge loss. As soon as I graduated from college, I made my way back to New York—and the fall—and now I never take this season for granted. I know what a world without fall feels like, and it's a dark place I hope I never return to. So when people ask me, "Why are you so obsessed with the fall?" I usually respond that absence does indeed make the heart grow fonder. And I am eternally very, very fond of this wonderful season we call fall.

Watching the abundant greenery in the driveway slowly transform into vibrant yellows and oranges is a truly magical experience.

SEPTEMBER

I will never forget the excitement of waking up on September 1st the first year after moving back to New York from Florida. I was twenty-seven years old, newly married, and working as the social media manager of a local e-commerce plumbing company. Most of the people who worked with me were also twenty-somethings, and 98% of them grew up in New York and Long Island. They were seasoned veterans of the fall and winter months—and they dreaded the cold that was inevitably on its way. You could only imagine their eye rolls when the new girl from Florida walked in on September 1st wearing a beanie and a sweater, with the look of a little kid who'd just met Santa Claus in her eyes. They were horrified by my appearance, asking me if I was aware it was still 80°F (27°C) outside, which I obviously was.

The way I see it, there's reality, and then there's my reality, and the two things do not necessarily line up in my mind. I love to romanticize my life, and stroll into every September 1st as if I am strolling into peak foliage, homemade pumpkin muffins, and endless pumpkin spice lattes. The anticipation of fall's arrival is almost better than living in it because there are so many days of fall left to live. I always, always miss the fall, even when I am still present in it—knowing that it is the time of year I look forward to the most. So by deciding the start of fall is on September 1st, I extend the greatest season of the year by a few weeks—and really, it isn't hurting anyone (except maybe myself, from overheating in flannels in 80°F weather).

ANTIQUE AUTUMN DÉCOR

My two biggest goals for my living room during September are to have as many pumpkin-scented candles as I can (so it smells like pumpkin pie and spices when people walk in) and to give my space a personalized and handmade feeling to it with as many DIY projects as I can! Homegoods and Target always come in clutch with adorable seasonal décor (that is affordable too), but there is something so special about adding in antiques and projects you've made by hand. I wanted to keep the A-frame living room free of any colors that felt too bright or saturated, and instead opted for a more subdued, neutral, and woodsy color scheme.

DIY

Painted Pumpkins

I transformed my favorite antique record stand from lush and green to witchy and autumnal by adding candlesticks, pine cones, and DIY painted pumpkins for a more personalized feeling. This project is so easy and can be done with your kids as well! You can, of course, paint any shape or pattern you desire. I chose to paint a ghost pattern on my orange pumpkins for a fun contrast.

You'll need:

Pumpkins, size of your choosing

Acrylic paint

Paint brushes

1. Paint the first color (white for the ghosts) onto your pumpkin in a pattern formation, trying to evenly space them around. Let this first coat dry completely.

2. Go back in with your second color (black for the ghosts). Use this second color to add any detail, (like the ghosts' eyes). Let the second coat dry completely. Then these can be added to any corner of your home to make it feel special!

PLAID AND PUMPKINS

As October comes closer, the jack-o-lantern pillows come out to play! I really love using patterns in this room, and the autumnal colored plaid pairs so nicely with the green tones in the A-frame wallpaper. Adding pops of orange brightened up the space, and lining the window with seasonal garland that lights up makes the space feels extra cozy at night.

FALL HARVEST

When it comes to pumpkins at my front door, my motto is always more is more! Of course, a more minimal entry design could also be cute because pumpkins are cute by nature, but I just love the overflowing look of pumpkins and mums, all mixed together, in all of my favorite colors! If you have a ledge, line it with mini pumpkins for an extra touch.

At the A-frame, I have a tiny little ledge above the door that I wanted to line with mini pumpkins, but the pumpkins were too wide to fit, so I sliced them in half. This gave the illusion of a bunch of full pumpkins over the door, which adds such a special touch. We also placed a mini pumpkin on the top of the railing to the steps. Like I said, more is more, and you just can't go wrong with pumpkins and mums everywhere!

Pumpkin Serving Tray

Every year when I host my fall party, I always seek creative ways to display my food that fits in with the fall theme. I usually serve a charcuterie board of various meats and cheeses on a wooden pumpkin charger, but I really wanted to have something with some height to display cookies this year, so I decided to make this serving tray. This was such an easy DIY, and it looked so adorable on the tablescape!

You'll need:

1 plastic pumpkin

Knife

Hot glue gun

Plate or tray

1. Cut the stem of the plastic pumpkin off using a knife, leaving a small hole on the top.

2. Hot glue the rim of the circle, then attach the plate on top of the pumpkin. That's it!

THE FALL PARTY

Every year, to celebrate the fall solstice, I host a fall party at my home in Long Beach. Everyone who attends is required to wear their favorite fall sweater and bring a homemade pie for a pie-tasting contest! I started this tradition because when I was younger, my mom would host a holiday party every year, and I remember how excited our entire family was the day before. I wanted to transfer this excitement into my own life as an adult, and thus the annual fall party was born.

I make sure to pick up every fall-themed piece of food that Trader Joes offers: ghost chips, pumpkin cookies, and orange-filled Oreos. I also grab all the timeless candies like candy corns, pumpkin-shaped candy corn, and gummy teeth. I like to offer a selection of every pumpkin beer that exists, or at least the ones my local beer store stocks, from Hudson North Cider Toasted Pumpkin to my personal favorite, Schlafly Pumpkin Ale. This isn't a Halloween party, rather, it's the time we gather to celebrate the official kickoff of fall. The best part has to be that my house has totally thrown up fall all over the place by the time the solstice arrives. There's nothing better than enjoying a fall-themed beverage while being surrounded with fall garlands and tiny pumpkins in every direction!

FROM SUNS TO PUMPKINS

The beauty of seasonal décor is that very small changes can make a huge difference. I am very attached to my orange duvet cover, so I wanted to hang onto it and transition it from summer to fall in September. During the summer months the bedroom has sun-patterned pillowcase covers and greenery overflowing from the open shelving. A quick change of the pillowcase covers from suns to pumpkins instantly makes the room feel ready for fall. I added a pumpkin-patterned throw blanket and some plaid throw pillows for more color and pattern, and some leaf garland along the frame of the bed as another touch. For the open shelving above the bed, I added some wood textures, vintage books, and candles to cozy up the space. Above the shelf I attached some faux leaves to the wall to give it a bit more dimension and color too.

To add a personalized touch to the space, I created a DIY pumpkin centerpiece to place next to my diffuser. The centerpiece also works on an entryway table, as a dining table centerpiece, and in so many other spots around your home. Here it adds another beautiful pop of orange to the bedroom.

On the fall solstice, the sun sets directly in line with the Long Beach boardwalk.
On this special night, when we walked to the ocean, the waves were offshore, and the sunset was as vibrant as it gets.

CIDER DONUT STAND

As I'm sure you've gathered about me by now, I am always looking for a reason to paint and repaint! I hated the idea that our summer lemonade stand would be sitting around unused during the fall and winter months, so I decided to repaint it and turn it into a cider donut stand. My 6-year-old loved the idea and got just as much of a thrill out of selling donuts as he did lemonade in the summer. I chose this red-orange color, and instead of painting over the lemonade sign at the top, I simply cut a new piece of wood to paint "Pumpkin" on, then drilled it on overtop. In summer, I can just unscrew it and swap out the signs, and we'll be back in business!

OCTOBER

I believe we can change our habits if we live consciously, but I also think so much of who we are and what we love comes from our childhood traditions. For me, it all started when I was a baby and my mom dressed me up as a cheerleader for my first Halloween. I had thick yellow strands of yarn to serve as hair atop my hairless head and a cute striped mini skirt, complete with pom-poms sitting next to me in every photo as an accessory. My mom decided that year, back in 1987, that she would make Halloween feel magical, and from that year on, she did just that. We never skipped dressing up or missed the chance to carve pumpkins during the month of October. When my brother Brian was born in 1988, she sewed us matching costumes. I was a clock and he was a cat, a play on Hickory Dickory Dock. When we were old enough to have our own opinions, we'd go to the costume store as a family and get to pick out what we wanted to dress up as. During my childhood years I was an old lady, a clown, Jeannie from *I Dream of Jeannie*, and so many more.

One year while we were carving pumpkins, I watched my brother's knife get stuck in his pumpkin, and when he tugged super hard to pull it out, it slid across his inner arm, slicing it open. My mom and littlest brother were inside, and I stood there in shock, watching the blood pour out as he walked around dripping it all over the pavement. It was truly a scene of gore, and it landed us in the emergency room on October 30th, resulting in 12 stitches on his inner arm. But that did not stop us from celebrating Halloween. We were committed to the holiday no matter what, and the very next day we were out trick-or-treating, stitches and all!

A year would not feel complete without carving a pumpkin and dressing up in a costume. I trick-or-treated until I was a senior in high school, and then when I moved to New York City for my freshman year of college at NYU, I remember buying a 12-pound pumpkin in Union Square. I walked the 10 blocks downtown with it in my hands, all the way back to my dorm. When my roommate asked me what I was doing, I told her that I could not *not* have a pumpkin! I carried on in this spirit all through college, being the friend who forced everyone to go to a pumpkin patch and carve a pumpkin with me.

My love for Halloween is as old as my time here on Earth, and other than my love for my own parents, I can't really think of anything else I've loved for this long. When the month of October comes, I am simultaneously so, so excited, and also so sad knowing how quickly it goes by and how soon it will be over. Once Halloween passes us by, I start the countdown for the next one on November 1st, planning my next costume and décor theme for most of the year leading up until Halloween greets us again.

Pumpkin Arch

The A-frame was meant to exist in October. Aside from the obvious color orange, something about the leaves scattered on the ground around it and the trees changing colors behind it lends it to feeling like an idyllic fall house. Leaning into that notion, I knew I had to go big for Halloween, even though it was unlikely any trick-or-treaters would find us out here in the woods. The A-frame would not feel complete for October unless it was decorated in an over-the-top way! I decided a DIY pumpkin arch was the perfect way to add lights, spook, and tons of pumpkins. The entire project took about a week of collecting pieces, and two days to fully assemble.

You'll need:

Plastic pumpkins with carved faces, battery operated with lights inside are preferred

White, black, and orange spray paint

PVC pipe: 3 straight pieces, 2 elbows

Drill

2 metal exterior hooks

Knife

Zip ties, 12in or longer

1 strand of white Christmas lights

Black feather garland

1. Spray paint your pumpkins with two coats of paint, allowing them to dry after each coat is applied.

2. Create the PVC pipe frame by connecting one straight piece (the top bar) to the other two straight pieces (the side bars) using the two elbows. The frame should look like a rectangle that is missing its bottom.

3. Drill your two hooks above the door—one on the left side and one on the right, so the top PVC pipe can sit within them. Secure the PVC frame in place.

4. Using a knife or a drill, cut three holes into the back of each pumpkin. Two holes are to weave the zip ties through to attach the pumpkin to the PVC pipe. The 3rd hole is to insert the Christmas lights inside the pumpkins so they light up if they do not come prelit.

5. Thread the zip ties through each of the pumpkins and begin attaching them to the PVC pipe. Start at the bottom on each side of the door and work your way up to the top. It's best to assemble the horizontal line of pumpkins over the door last.

6. Add the strand of Christmas lights into each pumpkin and weave them into the arch so they look discrete and the cord is not noticeable.

7. Using zip ties, attach the black feather garland to the PVC to add extra fullness to the arch. You can finish off the space by adding something fun like a skeleton and some additional pumpkins in the foreground.

PUMPKINS 25 C
For Sale

PUMPKINS IN THE WOODS

In Long Beach, I love to saturate my living room with bold orange garlands and bright-colored pumpkins in every nook and cranny. I wanted to go a different route at the A-frame and felt inspired by the theme of "pumpkins in the woods," which is a woodsy, toned-down fall color scheme that uses more neutrals, varying textures, DIYed garlands, branches, and candles. The palette is less vibrant, but it still feels super autumnal and cozy!

Jack-O-Lantern Coasters

This DIY is very kid friendly, and both of my sons helped me with it! You simply choose the design you'd like to have on the coaster and then begin gluing!

You'll need:
Hot glue gun
Cork coasters
1cm black and orange pom poms

1. Add the hot glue to the coaster and begin by creating the jack-o-lantern face using the black pom poms. If your kids are helping you with this DIY, it's a good idea for you to add the glue and let them place the pom poms.

2. Work your way up the circle, filling each section with a bit of hot glue and adding the orange pom poms to fill in around each jack-o-lantern face until you reach the full desired look.

MOODY SHOWER LIGHTING

When it comes to seasonal décor, bathrooms are often forgotten. Yet when you think about how much time we spend in our bathrooms daily, it's funny to think we wouldn't want them to feel a certain way. These are the spaces where we brush our teeth, shower, and get ready—the minutes add up! For Halloween specifically, I love to make the bathroom feel spooky by adding mood lighting from twinkle lights and candles.

SPOOKIFY

A quick and easy way to add some spook to your house that's low effort is by swapping out the pillows and blankets for October. I have a stash of ghost and pumpkin pillows that I pull out of hiding for this month, all of which are in the color scheme of orange and black. I generally steer clear of adding too much black into my décor, but in October, I like the drama it adds to a space.

I love to hoard tiny pumpkins from the local supermarket, since in my opinion, you can never add too many to the coffee table or side tables in your home. This year pumpkin-shaped pillows were trending, and I love having a few of them on the couch and around the floor to add more color into the space. You can finish the space off with more mini pumpkins, spooky candles, and some handmade jack-o-lantern coasters! My dog Claude is the cherry on top, outfitted in her spooky bat wings!

DRAMA IN THE KITCHEN

An easy way to add the drama of Halloween into a kitchen is by stringing some orange jack-o-lantern lights up along the shelves or cabinets. It makes the early mornings and late afternoons feel extra spooky! I also like to display some seasonal mugs to use for my morning coffee, which helps it feel festive. Alternating my ghost and pumpkin mugs on my wall hooks adds another fun touch to bring those Halloween vibes to life. I also love a countertop focal point that uses a wood round to place everything on, including a tiny pumpkin, a candle, and some seasonal décor. Having the candle burning while I cook brings about the delicious scent of pumpkin spice.

Witch Hats

Every year I try to push myself to find something creative to install above my soaker tub in Long Beach. The first year we moved in, I simply hung a banner and added some pumpkins on the floor. The second year I used fishing line and hung pumpkins from the ceiling. This year, I wanted to find something a little bit spookier. I kept seeing DIYers on the internet hanging witch hats above their entryways and realized this would be the perfect project for the bathroom. By hanging some remote control candles alongside the hats, I was able to take a soak at night, bathing in some dim, spooky lighting that was ideal for this season.

You'll need:

Witch hats

Sewing needle

Clear fishing line

Double-sided tape

Plastic candlesticks, battery operated

Command Hooks

1. Poke two holes at the top of each witch hat using a sewing needle. Thread the premeasured pieces of fishing line through the holes and secure the two ends of the fishing line to the ceiling with double-sided tape. Feel free to hang the witch hats at various heights.

2. Using the other pieces of premeasured fishing line, tie a loop around each candlestick. Double or triple knot the loop so it's securely attached. In my experience the double-sided tape is not strong enough to hold the candles, so I recommend using Command Hooks.

3. Place the Command Hooks at every spot on the ceiling you'd like to hang the candles from, and attach them with the fishing line onto the hooks. Tape any excess fishing line to the ceiling for both the witch hats and the candles. Adjust their spacing as necessary.

DIY

Flying Bats

When you put a little energy and love into a space, it goes from being forgotten about to a conversation piece. This is exactly the case with my stairwell! This corner looks very utilitarian when it's undecorated, but once I added these bats and lined the steps with mini pumpkins, it was completely transformed.

You'll need:

Pencil or pen

Bat designs to trace, 2 or 3 different sizes

Black construction paper

Scissors

Double-sided tape

1. Trace or draw your bat patterns on the black construction paper.

2. Layer three or four pieces of construction paper so you can cut out more than one bat at a time. Cut out as many bats as you'd like to display.

3. Attach the bats to the wall by placing two-sided tape in the center of each bat, and then fold the wings slightly, which will help them look like they're flying.

4. Place the bats onto the wall at varying heights in your desired location, and be sure the tape is pressed firmly onto the wall so they're secure.

A BEDROOM WITH PEAK FALL VIEWS

The leaves outside of the triangle window upstairs at the A-frame always influences the décor I bring into the space. In the summer, the leaves are bright, bold green. As they slowly shift to warm shades of oranges and yellows, I bring that same color into the bedroom by swapping out the bright white duvet for a more subdued shade of orange. Adding little pumpkins on the window ledge and on top of the beam is a small addition with a large impact. It's the coziest place to curl up with a book and watch the leaves slowly make their way from the tree down to the ground.

The only way to make the pumpkin arch even spookier was to pair it with a smoke bomb and a witch costume.

Every detail of the porch glows at night, including the pumpkin arch and the jack-o-lantern doormat that lights up when you step on it.

NOVEMBER

Like most things in life, the calendar year comes with its ups and downs. November 1st is undoubtedly always a down moment for me, and I am sure other Halloween lovers can relate. It is the day of the year that is the furthest away from Halloween, with 365 days to go. I wake up with a sugar hangover and a desire to pack up all of the Halloween decorations, but with a lot of exciting things to look forward to—the main thing being Thanksgiving!

I am lucky to call myself the host of my own family's Thanksgiving dinner, a title I've held for five years now. Once I gave birth to Hudson, traveling to Florida became difficult for Thanksgiving, so my parents and two brothers started traveling to me. There's something so exciting about knowing my entire immediate family will be spending a few days all together, especially since some years it is the only week that all five of us find ourselves under the same roof.

The first year of hosting, there was a lot I had to figure out, but by year five, our annual traditions have been set. There's something comforting about pulling out my wooden pumpkin chargers that we eat on every year, baking and cooking my mom's childhood recipes, and reminiscing on the year before in the same exact place with the same people. Coming together with my family for the Thanksgiving meal is so special.

FUNCTIONAL KITCHEN DÉCOR

Since I probably spend more time in my kitchen during the month of November than any other month, I try to find a nice balance of décor and function. There needs to be enough open counter space to cook meals for the kids on a daily basis, and for the big Thanksgiving meal, but with the right décor touches displayed throughout. Cooking Thanksgiving dinner in a fully decorated space makes the holiday feel even more celebratory.

A few swaps I make at the start of November:

- Change out the apron and dish towels on display

- Stock seasonal spatulas and spoons, and be prepared to use them

- Place some pumpkin scented candles on the kitchen counters so they're ready to light

- Create homemade fall garlands and hang them on the shelving

Apple Pie

Every year since moving back to New York, I go apple picking and come home with more apples than I know what to do with. I always end up using them in a delicious apple pie, the only kind of pie my dad and brothers will happily eat. (They're not big pumpkin pie fans, which I know is disturbing!) I like to make extra crust for little maple leaves to place on top for extra crunch! I've perfected this recipe over the years so the dough is perfectly crumbly, but not dry at all!

MAKES: one 9" pie // **TIME:** 3 hours

Crust:
- 1½ (210g) cups all-purpose flour
- ¼ cup (50g) pure cane sugar
- 1¼ tsp salt
- ¼ tsp baking powder
- 2¼ sticks butter, cold and cubed
- ½ cup (118ml) ice-cold water

Filling:
- 8–10 (650g) apples, peeled
- ½ cup (100g) pure cane sugar
- 6 tbsp dark brown sugar
- ¼ tsp salt
- ¼ tsp cinnamon
- 2 tbsp flour
- 2 tbsp cornstarch

1. In a stand mixer or in a large bowl if using a hand mixer, combine the flour, sugar, salt, and baking powder. Add in the butter and mix so all pieces have been broken down. Add in the ice-cold water and mix on medium until the dough begins to form.

2. Separate the mixed dough in half, and shape it into two disks. Refrigerate one half for the top and roll out the bottom. Once the dough is rolled out, fit it into the pie dish so it reaches all the way up the sides of the dish.

3. Preheat the oven to 400°F (204°C). While it preheats, place the rolled-out pie dough crust in the refrigerator for 30 minutes so it keeps its shape.

4. Make the filling by coring and slicing the apples, about ¼ inch thick. Add these into a large bowl, then mix in the rest of the dry ingredients. Stir to combine.

5. Let the filling sit at room temperature for about 30 minutes. The sugar will bring out the juices from the apples, so it's a good idea to strain most of the juices out so the pie doesn't get soggy.

6. Remove the crust from the refrigerator, and parbake for 20 minutes. Remove from the oven and let cool for 10 minutes. Lower the oven temperature to 350°F (177°C).

7. Add the filling to the bottom pie crust, and place the top layer of the crust overtop the filling to seal the pie. You can place it on the whole pie or make a lattice pie crust. Make sure there are slits on top so the steam can escape as the pie bakes.

8. Bake for 40 to 50 minutes, until the crust is golden brown. Add foil on top 25 to 30 minutes in to prevent the crust from burning. Remove from the oven and let cool for 30 minutes before serving.

Adding a plaid table runner and tall taper candles can completely transform a dining space for your Thanksgiving meal.

THANKSGIVING TABLE SETTING

Setting the Thanksgiving table is a job I do not take lightly. I love to mix up colors and textures, while also including some real pumpkins for a balanced, earthy, colorful tablescape. We always have a serve-yourself policy where we lay all the food out on the kitchen counter and everyone fills their own plate. This is an easier way to serve the meal since my dining room is somewhat tight and all of our food doesn't fit in the center of the table, especially with place settings for eight people.

DIY

Pumpkin Name Cards

This year I included a name card DIY using mini pumpkins that was a hit. It is an easy way to elevate your table for the Thanksgiving holiday.

You'll need:
Cardstock
Scissors
Black ink pen
Mini pumpkins
Gold push pins

1. Cut out rectangles from the cardstock, one for each guest. Make each rectangle a bit larger than what you want the final size to be.

2. To get a nice natural edge, tear off some of the paper on each side.

3. Use the pen to write each guest's name on a piece of cardstock.

4. Secure each name card to a mini pumpkin with a gold push pin. It's a good idea to wait until the morning of Thanksgiving to secure each name card to make sure the pumpkins don't spoil.

5. Place the pumpkin name cards at each place setting so your guests can easily find their seats.

AN AUTUMN-LOVER'S PARADISE

The benefit of an open-concept home is that it feels larger than it actually is, but with that comes the negative of having to be cognizant of the flow from one room into the other. This is the case with my dining room and living room. Knowing that my guests at Thanksgiving will also basically be seated in my living room, I love to carry over the warm, cozy, orange theme throughout the entire room. By utilizing plaids and thick-textured pillows, pumpkins, and leafy garlands, the entire living room feels like an autumn-lover's paradise.

WALK INTO FALL

I like to set the autumn scene for my house right
upon entry. Anyone who walks in will take the hint
that they've entered a fall vortex. I find that hanging
a leaf garland above the door adds a dramatic effect,
and I always hang a wreath on both the inside and
the outside. It depends on my mood, but I do
sometimes scatter fake leaves in the entryway if
I am feeling extra!

LITTLE PUMPKINS, ALL IN A ROW

When I travel to Vermont in the fall, especially in overly festive towns like Stowe, I notice that almost every house has pumpkins lining their fences and ledges. I took some inspiration from this and lined my own brick ledge in Long Beach with medium-sized pumpkins. I also use haystacks for height, and they hold up for months, all the way until my Christmas décor makes its way out.

This door color is inherently fall themed already, but if yours is not in the range of yellow or orange, a fun day project is to paint your door! My door is metal, which means I can't sand it down, but if you have a wood door, a quick sanding and some primer will get you set up to add a new color in no time.

POPS OF ORANGE

An easy and affordable way to sprinkle some pops of orange into the bathroom space is by simply adding pumpkins all around. I add some tiny pumpkins on top of the crossbeam, a tiny one next to my hand soap, and a few to line the floor. I add a pumpkin-scented candle next to the tub for easy lighting during an autumnal bath, and a quick swap of the runner for something orange and plaid helps make the space feel even more festive.

Seeing the leaves at their peak during fall is so fleeting, but it's a time that I look forward to all year. Having the gorgeous fall colors memorialized in photos makes the wait each year a little bit easier.

HOLIDAY

It's the most wonderful time of the year—and it is definitely the most everything else too! The most décor (just wait and see how festive each space can be!), the most dressing up, the most cooking, and the most time spent with family. It's always so full! I've always loved this about the end of each year, that after 12 months of working, learning, and growing, we all get to come together to finish off the year with a bang, dressed in our finest plaids while sipping on festive cocktails.

For the holiday season, it seemed like the A-frame was just itching to be covered in a giant bow, like the house itself is one of my greatest gifts because, really, it is! How lucky am I to be the owner of this adorable home? I found this oversized and weatherproof bow on QVC and attached it by drilling a couple of screws into the siding of our home, then I used the provided green gardening wire on the back of the bow to wrap it around the screws. For the garland, I used gardening wire to attach two strands together, which helped give it a fuller look. I threaded white Christmas lights throughout the garland after it was all securely attached. Our home looks so magical, especially all lit up at night, with the Christmas tree peeking out through one of the skylights, illuminating the living room.

I wanted our entry décor to be classic, so I chose this simple garland and wrapped it with lights.
It adds a beautiful glow as guests walk in at night!

DECEMBER

During the month of December, everyone is celebrating something. Maybe it's a holiday like Christmas or Hanukkah, a work promotion, or even just making it through another year! Reasoning aside, we're all either hosting or being hosted, welcoming our closest friends and family members into our space to share stories about our year, clink glasses, and exchange gifts. That holiday feeling always starts in our homes first, beginning with putting up a Christmas tree or stringing lights around window frames. These reflections warm up our living room each night as we run through our yearly lists of traditional holiday movies. Home décor plays such a large role in getting us into the holiday spirit, and every special touch might be the one thing your guests remember about your home for years to come.

There's a home around the block from me that takes this time every year to set up a beautiful light display out front. It has become a huge part of our December tradition to drive past this house every night when the lights turn on, and to slowly take in each special detail. We don't know the homeowner, and we don't live on their block, but the effort they put into their front lawn adds to our December magic every year.

It's the little things that make friends and family feel the most special, things like pulling out the reindeer glassware with the gold rim for cocktails, bringing homemade cookies to a holiday party, or lighting candlesticks at dinnertime with the overhead lights dimmed. My home feels like magic during the month of December, and I cherish watching my loved ones' eyes light up as they step inside and are greeted with delicious smells, an overwhelming amount of lights and garlands, and a glass of eggnog waiting for them on the counter.

NEVER TOO MUCH GARLAND

The theme of my living room is "never too much garland," and I am proud to say I think I accomplished the goal. Since my house is surrounded by woods, I love feeling like I can bring some of that into our Christmas décor with garland surrounding the double doors and the mirror, and strung along most of the beams. I also add in an abundance of twinkle lights, lining the walls with remote-control firefly lights that disappear when turned off but add a touch of magic when they're on. I owned these A-Frame stocking holders before I had the home, so it only felt fitting to incorporate them into our mantle for the holiday season.

A SIMPLE SCANDINAVIAN-INSPIRED TREE

Most of our sentimental ornaments are stored in our Long Beach home, so for our tree at the A-frame we opt for a simple, Scandinavian-inspired look. Using light wood garland, and a sparse amount of ornaments that have a silver antique look, the simplicity of the tree is a nice contrast to the rest of the space which is filled to the brim with ornaments and décor. It's a perfect place to gather, and we've often had close friends come over on the day after Christmas to open gifts and sit around the fireplace while the kids play with their new toys.

STOCKED HOT COCOA BAR

There's nothing quite as cute as a hot cocoa bar on your kitchen counter for snowy days. It's fun for the kids and the grownups too! I like to keep mine stocked with Hershey's chocolate bars, marshmallows, and snowman pops to dip into our mugs. I added a pine cone garland to the open shelving for some winter textures. This is an easy-to-make garland you can DIY yourself with just a few items.

The green of our cabinetry looks so lovely paired with classic red plaids. Adding some garland around the window gives the kitchen the coziest, Christmassy feeling. I also swapped out my oven mitt for this adorable hunter green one, covered with candy canes all over.

To make our dining room feel more seasonally appropriate, I like to add a wreath on the back of each chair, paired with red plaid cushions for the seats.

PATTERN PLAY

I absolutely love the marriage of the A-frame wallpaper with the red plaid comforter for the month of December. It makes our guest room feel like a cozy Christmas North Pole cabin, especially with the addition of lit alpine trees in the corner of the room and lit garland surrounding the window. When installing the A-frame wallpaper, I loved the idea that it would work well in all seasons. I impatiently waited to see how beautiful the green would translate during the holidays. I found it works perfectly during December, acting as a neutral background, while still adding some color into the room.

SANTA MUG COLLECTION

I love my kitchen décor most during the holidays. I've been collecting Santa mugs throughout the years, and I decorate my open shelving with these mugs that are special to me. I also love to add garland to every open shelf, above my cabinetry, and around the window to make the space smell delicious, and feel extra Christmassy!

DIY

Santa Napkin Rings

This DIY is so cute and unexpected at a Christmas dinner. It requires very little, other than a hint of planning ahead when ordering the jewel for the belt. Everything else can be picked up at a local craft store. Paired with a neutral or red napkin, it is such a cute way to dress up a table.

You'll need:

Leftover paper towel or toilet paper roll
Paintbrush
Red acrylic paint
Scissors
Hot glue gun
White and black ribbon
Square jewel

1. Paint the rolls red. You'll want to paint two layers for an even covering.

2. When the paint is completely dry, cut the rolls down to the desired size you'd like your napkin holders to be.

3. Hot glue the white ribbon along the two edges of each roll you're making.

4. If your jewel needs to be strung through the black ribbon, be sure to do so before gluing the black ribbon on. Then hot glue the black ribbon around the center of each roll. If your jewel can be added on last, hot glue it to the center of the black ribbon belt once it's attached.

5. Pull your favorite festive napkins through the finished napkin rings and display on your table setting!

Festive Sugar Cookies

Aside from the requirement of Santa needing a cookie to take a bite out of on Christmas Eve, there is something special about showing people you love them with delicious homemade cookies. I love to have a cookie decorating night with my kids where we paint and add sprinkles to cookies however they like. I also like to make my own where I get really perfectionist with all the cute gingerbread outfits and candy canes. This recipe is delicious, and the cookies keep their shape in the oven.

Makes: 2 dozen // **Time:** 2 hours

Ingredients:

2¼ cups (315g) all-purpose flour

½ tsp baking powder

¼ tsp salt

¾ cup (170g) unsalted butter, softened

¾ cup (150g) granulated sugar

1 large egg

2 tsp pure vanilla extract

¼ tsp almond extract

Icing:

3 egg whites

1 lb (450g) confectioners' sugar

1 tsp pure vanilla extract

1. In a medium-size bowl, mix together the flour, baking powder, and salt. Set aside.

2. In a large bowl, using a hand or stand mixer, beat the butter and sugar together until smooth. Add the egg, vanilla, and almond extract, and beat until combined.

3. Slowly fold in the dry ingredients and mix on low until they are well combined. The dough should be a bit sticky, but still malleable.

4. Separate the dough into two disks, wrap both in plastic wrap, and refrigerate for 1 to 2 hours. Once the dough is chilled, preheat the oven to 350°F (176°C).

5. Line two baking sheets with parchment paper. Pull the dough out of the refrigerator, and let it soften for a bit, about 10 to 15 minutes.

6. Dust a work surface with flour, and roll out the dough into about 1/4-inch thickness.

7. Using cookie cutters, cut the dough into shapes. Continue until all of the dough has been used. Place the cookies about 2 inches apart on the cookie sheet so they won't touch once they expand in the oven.

8. Bake for about 15 minutes if they are standard gingerbread size. Bake for slightly less time if they are smaller.

9. Let the cookies cool for at least 10 minutes.

10. To make the icing, using a hand mixer or stand mixer, beat the egg whites on medium-low speed until frothy, about 1 minute.

11. With the mixer on low speed, slowly add in the confectioners' sugar and vanilla until fully incorporated, and then increase the speed to medium and beat until stiff peaks form.

12. Divide the icing among small bowls and dye with food coloring if desired. Transfer to piping bags, and decorate the cookies.

CHRISTMAS EVE TABLE SETTING

A tartan tablecloth can take a plain white table to festive in just seconds! I placed a bow on the back of each chair using Command Hooks and ribbon, adding adorable pops of red that tie into the tablecloth. If you happen to have leftover candy canes lying around, you can hot glue three of them together so they stand on their own to create an easy place card holder for seating.

Cabinet Wreaths

If your entire home is decorated, sometimes it's hard to find ways to integrate that décor into your kitchen in a unique way. One idea is to dress up your cabinets like I've done here. It adds so much life and color to an otherwise all-white corner of my house!

You'll need:

Command Hooks

Red bows

Mini 8-inch wreaths

Twist ties

Ribbon

1. Secure a Command Hook to the top inside of each cabinet door you plan to hang a wreath on.

2. Attach the red bows to the bottom of the 8-inch wreaths with twist ties.

3. String a long piece of ribbon through each wreath, and tie a knot at the end when you decide on your desired length.

4. Loop the knotted ends into the Command Hooks inside your cabinets, and adjust as necessary so each wreath hangs at your desired height

A MAGICAL PLACE FOR HOLIDAY SLUMBERS

When I started to see the trend of homes with multiple Christmas trees, I just knew I wanted to fall asleep next to the twinkle of a tree in my bedroom. I felt the same way about adding some holiday magic into my closet since I spend a lot of time in there getting ready for holiday parties and filming holiday styling videos. White Christmas lights illuminate my favorite holiday sweaters—some vintage, some from my favorite kitschy brand KJP, and others I've collected over the years. I add some alpine trees with lights on them too, so at night my closet has a warm glow to it whenever I come home.

A RED FRONT DOOR FOR CHRISTMAS

I joke around that I repaint my front door for every season, but lately I am starting to wonder if it is actually a joke. I truly do repaint my door as the weather shifts, and this year, I felt like red was necessary for the Christmas season. It looks so nice paired with green garland and the giant red bows on the steps!

DIY

New Year's Eve

Dressing up on New Year's Eve is so fun, and there's nothing like coming prepared with crowns and noisemakers! This year, I felt like the offering for New Year's crowns just wasn't cutting it for me. I wanted something bigger with more glitter and larger numbers. I looked all over and could not find what I was envisioning, so I decided to make it myself. It looks so cute in photos to ring in the new year.

You'll need:

Scissors	Marker or pen
Store-bought crown	Glitter paper
	Hot glue

1. Cut off the lettering on the original crown if there is any.

2. Mark the width of the crown onto the back of the glitter paper so you know how wide you need your numbers to be.

3. Once you decide on the width, write out the numbers of the year, then cut them out.

4. Hot glue them onto the original crown, and you're done!

The sun sets by 4 p.m. during the week of Christmas at the A-frame, but it's hard to be mad about it when the fire is roaring and the house feels so warm and cozy.

ACKNOWLEDGMENTS

Thank you, thank you, thank you to all the supportive, kind, inspiring internet strangers from across the world who I consider my friends. Without your comments, shares, views, and interest in my A-frame, the opportunity for this book would not have made its way to my inbox or to the eyes of Alexander Rigby's TikTok for you page!

Thank you to Alexander Rigby, my editor, for believing in me and giving me the opportunity to create a version of my internet persona that I can hold in my own two hands. Without the trust and belief that he had in me, this book would not have been possible.

Thanks to my husband, Matt, for loving the A-frame at first sight as much as I did and for jumping into the process of buying it and renovating it with me.

Thanks to my dad for ripping out our deck with his own two hands, insulating our crawl space to keep us warm all winter long, and being my number-one supporter in every DIY project that I was unsure I could make happen. And to my mom for showing me

that decorating for the holidays makes a house feel more like a home.

Thanks to Sea for spending hours upon hours of painting, styling, photographing, and suffering through Taylor Swift albums while we fixed up the house and prepped for all the photo shoots. Thanks to Nick for jumping headfirst into every seasonal shoot, even if it involved traveling hours away during a blizzard. Thanks to Alain for instilling in me a solid work ethic at a young age and showing me that confidently trying new things is how we make ourselves better. And thanks to Amanda for guiding me every step of the way.

Thanks to my two wonderful sons, Hudson and Charlie. Thanks to Aunt Elisa, Uncle Pat, and my in-laws, Sheryl and Curt. Thanks to Brian, Matt, Dana, and Sammy for always being there. And thanks to the best friends: Noelle, Alex, Sara, and Erin.

Lastly, thanks to DK and Penguin Random House for taking a chance on me and making my dreams of writing a book come true!

Photo shows the team at the summer shoot. Left to right: Sea D'Amico, Amanda Acevedo, me and Claude, Nick Glimenakis, Jessica Lee, and Alexander Rigby.

Drawing above created by my six-year-old son Hudson to show the A-frame through the seasons.

INDEX